S0-BOP-137

FACTS

and

FAITH

VOLUME II

THE BIBLE AND FAITH

By J. D. THOMAS

Published by
Biblical Research Press
774 East North 15th Street
Abilene, Texas 79601

FACTS AND FAITH
Volume II

By J. D. Thomas

Copyright ©, 1980, by
BIBLICAL RESEARCH PRESS

Library of Congress Catalog Card No.
I.S.B.N. 0-89112-012-2

All rights in this book are reserved. No
part of it may be reproduced in any
manner without permission of the
author except brief quotations used in
connection with a review in a magazine
or newspaper.

To Katherine —

a beautiful soul

FOREWORD

We apologize for being so long in getting this volume out. Our intentions were good but we are only human and have many limitations. We have also permitted some other writings to get in ahead of this one because at the time they seemed to be more deserving of immediate attention. We hope that the delay will prove justified in the quality of the book.

The encouragement we have received about getting this volume out and the numerous inquiries about it have made us see that its writing was a "must," and we are grateful for such encouragement.

This volume, more so than Volume I, is a deliberate "apologetic" in its approach. Both volumes were written in the hopes of "making believers," but we dealt with the more technical material in the first book and in this we felt the need to be persuasive. Every author has an objective for which he hopes to win followers, and we certainly are not "ashamed of the gospel." We have no apologies for asking people to believe with all their hearts that God is, that Christ is his Son, that the Holy Spirit is active in God's will, that the Bible is God's word, and that the church of the New Testament is his family.

Our obligations are numerous — for helpful ideas in certain areas — to Bill Davis on *Freewill*, Carl Brecheen on *Self-Esteem*, and any number of my former teachers and to books from which I have learned. Thanks to Martha Renfro for typing the manuscript.

Abilene, Texas
Christmas 1979

CONTENTS

VOLUME II

THE BIBLE AND FAITH

INTRODUCTION

FACTS AND FAITH

Vol. II

THE BIBLE AND FAITH

INTRODUCTION

CHAPTER 1

REVELATION, AUTHORITY AND FAITH

People in Christian contexts often speak of the Bible as *revelation,* they often speak of the *authority* of the Bible, and they practically take for granted *faith* in the Holy Scriptures as God's divine rule for faith and practice. Differing theological emphases however look at these factors differently, but most "Christian" views use each of these terms seriously in their relation to each other. They are terms that have had a strong influence in all the ages of Christian history. For a clear understanding of what is meant by Christianity, it is imperative that we define these terms properly and especially that we understand their relation to each other.

Authority is one avenue of knowing. Other possible avenues are *Reason, Experience* (empiricism), and, as some would say, *Intuition,* but most of what the average man of today accepts as truth is learned by him from an *Authority,* through revelation or testimony, and is accepted by faith. The *Authority* can be God himself or any person who has empirically (through one of his five senses) experienced a truth. He tells others (revelation), who accept his statement as true (faith), and which they then accept as valid knowledge. By way of illustration, we have all learned most of what we know from a teacher, who received his knowledge either empirically, or from other teachers, who then ultimately trace their knowledge back to someone who had an original empirical experience. The apostles actually *saw* Christ after the resurrection, and they committed their testimony "to faithful men who shall be able to teach others also" (2 Tim. 2:2) and thus it has come on down to us.

The Need for Propositional Revelation

A revelation from an authority needs to be propositional. This means that the testimony should be in cognitive, information-bearing statements that can be clearly understood by the receiving minds. "Better felt than told," mystical feelings do not qualify. They must be in communicable language, should carry public truth, so that all can know the same exact revelation from the same propositional statements.

For centuries the Bible was recognized as a propositional-statement revelation, but in the last two hundred years there has been a reaction against reason, and, then later, another reaction against even the hard facts of scientific knowledge, so that there is today a growing appreciation of subjectivity and inwardness — of a more private, non-communicable knowledge, thanks to Existentialism, Phenomenology and other recent views that defend subjectivity. This new mood tends to bypass the intellect of man in favor of his will and emotions. Reason is negated and the supposed "knowledge" which ensues is therefore not related to fact or logic. There is nothing to give assurance that mere superstition, wishful thinking, or perhaps imagination, is not what is being accepted.

Propositional-word revelation provides a gospel message (see Romans 10:17) which can be preached and believed, and which in time yields a noticeably new and changed life — available to all men everywhere on the same terms, and thus a public, objective truth. Anything different from the clear message of the gospel which can be understood, believed, obeyed, and lived out in one's life cannot be what the Bible offers.

A clear revelation in propositional-word statements is therefore a must, but this is exactly what the Bible is.

THE BIBLE AS VALID
RELIGIOUS AUTHORITY

CHAPTER 2

THE CHALLENGE OF HIGHER CRITICISM

For seventeen hundred or more years after the New Testament was completed the Bible was counted as valid religious authority in practically all circles that considered themselves Christian. Modern "Higher Criticism" however has changed this. Several factors in history have contributed to this state of affairs, but chief among them has been the rise of science and a consequent overweening appreciation of the basic philosophy of Naturalism.

During the time of the lack of education of "the Dark Ages," men believed strongly in supernatural activity in the world, and they felt that God made immediate decisions for every event — for example, when the weather changed. When learning and education began to rise again, secular influences and secular thinking came to be highly respected. Thomas Aquinas (13th century A.D.) exercised enough influence as philosopher and theologian to get people to accept the idea that "philosophy precedes faith." Biology, for instance, can be studied apart from any immediate theological implications. Secular concerns need not be tied to theological concerns.

When Martin Luther later challenged the pope and the general councils of the church as infallible authorities, it shook the thinking people, who then came to feel that they needed a new source of authority. Luther held that this should be the Bible, with the Holy Spirit guiding each individual man in his interpretation. His conclusion was rejected by many, but accepted by others.

About this time, modern science began to arise and it also brought a new way of looking at things. Francis Bacon introduced a clear statement of the inductive method of reasoning, and this eventually became "the Scientific Method," when coupled with the contributions of Newton and Galileo, plus higher mathematics, precision measurements and with an attitude of thoroughness.[1]

---

[1]For a fuller treatment of this development see Chapters 13 and 14 of *Facts and Faith*, Volume I.

A Naturalistic, "Scientism" Matrix

The upshot of all the new post-Reformation thinking was that "nature" was now appreciated more than ever. "Natural law" became a commonly used concept, as it came to be realized more than ever before that nature worked uniformly and in definite cause-effect relationships. This new view brought a drastic change to philosophy, and Naturalism came to dominate many circles as the primary basic philosophy or world-view. If all events can be explained as the result of natural causes, then God is not necessarily "up there pushing the buttons," and as a consequence of this thought, many people decided that we do not really need God at all.

Admittedly science and the scientific method have provided great gains for mankind. Scientific knowledge peculiarly builds upon itself — that is, all the new scientific knowledge learned becomes "building blocks" or new data for the learning of even more knowledge. Thus in the three hundred years that science has been with us, it has by now provided so many inventions and discoveries that our way of life and thinking have gone through several major revolutions. Color TV and antibiotics, for example — which would have been considered as miracles a few generations earlier — are now quite commonplace, and they are considered to be very simple concepts in the thinking of today's research scientists. There is no telling what science may do for us in the next hundred years.

The new scientific learning then led to the desire on the part of some theologians to want to update their own field of knowledge, so that they, too, could attract the notice of the world with similar new gains in religious learning. This desire logically called for a repudiation of many of the older, traditional beliefs. This attitude also developed into the rejection of all supernatural concepts in favor of "everything happening naturally." Miracles, inspiration, and other supernatural activities recorded in the scriptures all finally came to be rejected by the new "modern" thought, and Christianity in its entirety has now come to be interpreted by these "Modernists" or "Liberals" completely in terms of naturalism. One trouble with this new approach is that when one completely cuts out the supernatural from the Biblical revelation he does not even have a "skeleton" left. The Bible is a book relating numerous supernatural deeds, interwoven with normal history. God can and does intervene providentially in natural events as he sees the need. There is no demanding reason to discount the supernatural if one can believe in God at all. No miracle in the Bible is beyond a logical, reasonable faith. The God who made natural law need not be absolutely bound by it. The use of supernaturalism is possible.

Pre-rejection of the Supernatural

This *naturalistic* attitude of Liberalism in the study of the Bible caused the rise of what we call "Higher Criticism." This term in practicality has come to mean "a scientific study of the Bible from the basic philosophical stance of naturalism." The *subject matter* studied by "Criticism" is valid and is not a problem. Conservative scholars study these matters just the same as Liberal scholars — such considerations as dates, authorship, purposes, historical facts, and numerous other topics. The real difference between Liberal and Conservative Bible scholars is the philosophical presupposition with which each begins, and which generally determines their final conclusions. The Liberal works from the point of view of naturalism, while the Conservative has no trouble accepting the possibility of supernatural deeds as may be recorded in the Bible — miracles, inspiration, and such like.

Well-known conclusions of naturalistic Higher Critics include:

- A denial of Mosaic authorship of the Pentateuch, in favor of "an evolution of ideas" and a "documentary hypothesis" for the development of these five books of Moses.

- The Synoptic Gospels are not historically dependable for a true picture of Jesus.

- No miracle has ever happened. Everything must be explained otherwise.

- There are many factual and historical discrepancies in Scripture.

- The Bible was written for its own age only, and is therefore not self-consciously a book of Scripture for all ages.

- The church was not consciously built by Jesus, but is an afterthought on the part of his disciples.

- Jesus is not the Son of God, but at best was only a religious genius — maybe not even a remarkable person.

- The Bible is the world's best book, but is in no way an authoritative revelation of God's will for men of today. It has some good teachings and moral principles, but each man must choose for himself and thus finally be his own authority.

CHAPTER 3

ALLEGED DISCREPANCIES OF THE BIBLE?

In giving a title to this chapter, we use the word "alleged" because of the strong charge by critics that there are such discrepancies, while other scholars insist that there are no real discrepancies — what is at question are only "apparent" discrepancies. The seeking scholar can find sufficient explanation, and it is only the superficial reader or the antagonistic reader who thinks the problems are real, so the argument goes.

That there are "apparent" problems or difficulties there is no doubt, but in the view of this writer such difficulties need not mitigate against Christian faith. The atheist or skeptic also lives by a faith (no one *knows* all truth), and every person has problems in connection with the faith that he chooses to live by. *Absolute certainty* is not possible in this life about either present spiritual realities or life beyond the grave; therefore, every person has to select one of the alternative faiths that are open to men. "We walk by faith, and not by sight" (2 Cor. 5:7). You can believe in the God of creation, or you can put your faith in nature and mere chance. Either way, you do not *know* for sure what the explanation of human existence is, and whichever faith you choose to follow will have some problems or difficulties. If this were not so, we could all eventually figure out the right faith which has no problems and then we would follow it. Believers could force atheists to change (or vice versa), by logic.

So, the existence of problems is not insurmountable. Indeed this fact might be a means of strengthening faith. Certainly problems lend to the excitement of determining what our faith shall be.

History

Since the second century, A.D., the Bible has been accused of having contradictions or discrepancies. Practically every point raised in this connection today was raised in the days of the early church. No new facts are produced. Yet Christian faith has continued on, unabated, for two thousand years, so it would seem that there are no real problems that need cause one to reject the God of the Bible nor the Bible as His revealed will.

9

Scholars of the early church knew of these same problems, which were raised back then, and they studied them and answered the critics of that day. Justin Martyr (ca. 160 A.D.) said, "I am convinced that no Scripture contradicts another" (Dialogue with Trypho, ch. 65). Irenaeus, the first "church father" (ca. 180 A.D.) said, "the Scriptures are indeed perfect since they were spoken by the word of God and his Spirit." (Against Heresies II, 28, 2). Similar statements can be found in the writings of other notable early scholars. Celsus and Porphyry are probably the best known of the early Biblical critics, and although they marshalled many of the same arguments used today against the integrity and authority of the Bible, they were not successful in their challenge. Christianity mushroomed, right in the face of their efforts.

Design

In view of all the facts and information to be considered in accepting any faith, it is not surprising that faith in the Bible as God's word should have problems that call for investigation and study. In fact, this could well be a part of God's design, in that problems cause the study of the Scriptures, more than they would otherwise be studied. They are a stimulus to the intellect. Study thus engendered brings the realization that surely here are wonderful writings — too wonderful for man to have produced alone. A respect for the Bible is produced in the open-minded truthseeker, who feels he must "find the answer" when a possible discrepancy is noted. He learns much of the word of God while searching its pages, and so the problems become a means of instruction for him. Again, they serve as a stumbling block for the skeptic. 2 Thess. 2:10-12 indicates that God permits a "working of error" to be sent to those who "love not the truth," and thus their "believing a lie" becomes the basis for their final condemnation. A truthseeker must be honest and open-minded, without bias or prejudice. He must be willing to follow where truth leads.

Further, the apparent discrepancies show that there was no collusion between the Biblical writers. Had they *planned* to defraud humanity they would have covered over some of the apparent problems that we now find.

The Issues

The importance of whether Biblical "discrepancies are real" is viewed differently by different theological groups. *Liberals* count them as real and therefore as rendering the Bible as completely undependable for being God's word on a "chapter and verse" basis. *Neo-Orthodox* or existentialist theologians follow the same view toward the Bible as Liberals. Their presuppositions do not need an external, public authority anyway, since they hold that God "reveals" to each man in a private, subjective way.

Evangelicals comprise the largest group of American Protestants, and these, though generally defenders of the integrity and authority of the word, today find themselves divided into groups, particularly on the question of Biblical "inerrancy." At the current writing, there is among the Evangelicals a "Battle for the Bible," with the prime issue being whether there can be real discrepancies or errors and a valid faith still be maintained.

John Calvin (1509-1564) believed in an "internal persuasion of the Holy Spirit" for the certainty that the Bible is God's word, and he argued that one cannot know that the Bible is God's word "without faith" (Institutes 1. 8. 13). Thus for Calvin the word is dependent upon faith (though Romans 10:17 says "faith comes by hearing and hearing by the word of Christ" rather than the word being dependent upon faith). In Calvin's case, therefore, apparent discrepancies are of no concern, since he believed that the Holy Spirit told him personally and directly that the Bible *is* God's word. The authority for him is *his* experience with the Spirit, and the impact of the word itself therefore becomes negligible. Even though one might not be able to explain a difficulty, Calvin's faith that it is of no consequence is maintained, due to his complete dependence upon his experience with the Spirit. Many Evangelicals of today hold to this view — namely, that there are discrepancies, but still the Bible is God's word since the Spirit has so declared it. One just does not need to get "all that concerned" about possible problems.

Other Evangelicals reject such a strong "inner witness of the Spirit" on this question and feel that they get their authority from *the personal Christ*. The Christ himself had strong faith in the Scriptures and declared them to be authoritative, thus they are. In substance this view is the same as the one above. The source of knowledge is different — the one reveals by an inner witness of the Spirit, while the other comes through propositional words of Jesus, but in both cases the authority is supernatural and is there. Yet in both views the power of the word by itself, after it is inscripturated, seems to be diminished.

Many Biblical texts declare that *the word itself* carries spiritual power, e.g.:

> Rom. 1:16 - For I am not ashamed of the gospel: it is the power of God for salvation to everyone who has faith, . . .

> James 1:21 - . . . receive with meekness the implanted word, which is able to save your souls.

> Psalm 119 - (Includes 176 verses similar to vs. 2 - Blessed are those who keep his testimonies, who seek him with their whole heart, . . .)

> 1 Cor. 4:15 - . . . I became your father in Christ Jesus through the gospel.

It would seem that *if* the Bible is God's word, given in propositional, logical statements, no additional inspiration of supernatural power should be needed for the normal man to comprehend its teaching for himself. Indeed, if additional impact is needed in the form of "inner witness" or through a specially empowered or ordained priest, one could logically ask what is the benefit of the inspiration of the word itself in the first place? Surely more than one supernatural expression is not necessary. If it were, this would challenge the effectiveness of inspiration. The Scriptures themselves recognize no weakness, but rather claim an infallibility which must not be tampered with (Gal. 1:8, 9.[2]

---

[2]The citation by "inner-witness' advocates of 1 Corinthians 2:11-15, "natural man" versus "spiritual man," *et cetera*, is not germane to their conclusion since the context (vs. 7f) shows that the "mystery" is God's plan of salvation, now revealed through inspired men, but unrecognizable by carnally minded men who have no spiritual appreciation, and who do not seek spiritual growth. There is no indication here of Calvinistic unconditional election and the domination by spiritual control of men who are non-seekers. "Faith comes by hearing" the gospel and accepting its truth (Romans 10:17)!

A real issue concerning discrepancies asks whether there are errors in Scripture in the central matters of faith and morals, or whether they are found only in matters of scientific and historical fact, but also whether the two groups are so interwoven that they cannot be separated. If there are errors in science and history, how could the average man be sure that there are none in faith and morals, and how can he distinguish clearly between them? If we can't trust the Bible on some statements, how can we trust it in others? If one denies the inerrancy of Scripture, where shall he find a "Thus said the Lord" that he can depend on? Is he not apt to go into Existentialism or some other form of subjectivity?

Kenneth Kantzer, right after he became editor for the prominent evangelical magazine, *Christianity Today*, said,

> Rather, evangelicals must show that *it is just because we believe the autographs were inerrant* that we have an objective path to truth. The assurance that we possess the correct text (on the basis of the objective and public data of textual criticism) plus the assurance that we possess the true meaning of the Scripture (on the basis of the objective and public data of grammar and syntax and usage) provides for the inerrantist the support of his conviction that he has the truth of God.[3]

Kantzer's is thus a mediating view between the present conflicting evangelical views. He himself comes out strong for the need for an acceptance of the fact of inerrancy, otherwise you would have no way for an objective knowledge of God's truth. Carl F. H. Henry, founding editor of *Christianity Today* and prominent evangelical theologian, commits himself to inerrancy, and he also takes a mediating position in the current tensions between Evangelicals. Henry seems to be strong for the power inherent in the word itself, in that in his new four-volume *magnum opus, God, Revelation and Authority*, he says,

> Divine revelation is the source of all truth, the truth of Christianity included; reason is the instrument for recognizing it; scripture is its verifying principle; logical con-

---

[3]Editorial, *Christianity Today*, April 21, 1978.

sistency is a negative test for truth and coherence is a subordinate test. The task of Christian theology is to exhibit the
content of Biblical revelation as an orderly whole.[4]

Types of Difficulties

As a matter of checking into types of difficulties that
different authors have found, John W. Haley lists the following:

- Difference of dates of passages
- Differences of authorship
- Different methods of arrangement
- Different methods of computation
- Peculiarities of Oriental idiom
- Plurality of names or synonyms
- Diverse meanings of the same word
- Errors in the manuscripts
- Imagination of the critic[5]

R. A. Torrey's list includes:

- Those that arise from the text in the original languages
- Those that arise from inaccurate translations
- Those that arise from false interpretations
- Those that arise from a wrong conception of the Bible
- Those that arise from the original languages themselves
- Those that arise from our defective knowledge of
  history, geography and customs of Bible times
- Those that arise from ignorance of conditions under
  which books were written and commands given
- Those that arise from the many sidedness of the Bible
- Those that arise from the fact that the Bible is infinite
  while our minds are finite
- Those that arise from the dullness of our spiritual
  perceptions[6]

There are overlappings among these types of problems as
listed, but in totality they indicate that there could well be many

---

[4]Vol. I, *God Who Speaks and Shows: Preliminary Considerations*, p. 215.
[5]*Alleged Discrepancies of the Bible*, Nashville: B. C. Goodpasture, Reprint, 1951, Chs. I,
II, III.
[6]*Difficulties in the Bible*, New York: Fleming Revell Co., 1907, pp. 29-121.

of them that are explainable, and thus they need not indicate that there are real errors or true, unsolvable discrepancies. One person may not read a text exactly, or may not be aware of different possible principles of arrangement or of the purpose of point of view of the author. Figurative language can be a source of misunderstanding, and the fact that there are different modes of reckoning time no doubt accounts for several problems. It may be that in a given situation the author did not purpose to give all of the facts or even give them in their chronological order. This is no doubt true in many of the variations between the gospel records of the life and activities of Jesus.

Eminent jurists are slow to reject diametrically contradictory testimony in a jury trial. The different standpoints and backgrounds of the witnesses may be the basis for harmonizing the evidence, so they seek additional information, without deciding at once that the testimony is irreconcilable. As we view the alleged discrepancies in the Bible, we should realize that all the evidence is not in, and new archaeological or other evidence may someday clarify a problem completely. To be sure, the religious and moral values of the Bible are not impaired by the presence of difficulties. Most of us are acquainted with paradoxes, where two seemingly opposite statements can well both be true at the same time, when each is properly understood.

Faith in the Bible as God's word therefore need not be seriously challenged by the presence of problems, as indeed history has improved. Faith has prospered in spite of full awareness of difficulties.

Illustrations

Textual variations are the most common source of apparent discrepancies, and Textual Criticism is the method scholars use to determine the original wording of the manuscripts. Both conservative and critical scholars accept this method as valid and necessary. The findings of Textual Criticism have served to clarify many problems and they show that textual variants are ultimately of no serious significance. I. M. Price, a critical scholar, says of the New Testament, "Only four hundred or so of the 150,000 variants materially affect the sense, and of these, perhaps fifty are of real significance. But no essential teaching of the New Testament is greatly affected by them."[7]

One problem that Textual Criticism has solved is found in 2 Chronicles 3:3, 4, where Solomon's temple is described as being twenty cubits wide, sixty cubits long, and one hundred twenty cubits high. Such a building would be quite a monstrosity. 1 Kings 6:2 says that the height of Solomon's temple was only thirty cubits. Both of these references are from the Hebrew text, but when we turn to the Greek text of 2 Chronicles 3:4 we find that the building is only thirty cubits high. Thus, by comparing the several texts of the passage and using a modicum of common sense, it is easy to see that one of the Hebrew copyists simply made an error in copying, and the difficulty is no problem at all for faith. No one believes that God inspired copyists of Scripture, only the authors of the original manuscripts. To believe in inspired copying would mean that one could not copy Scripture today and make an error.

Numbers furnish a source for several difficulties in Scripture. The wilderness wanderings of the people of God coming out of Egypt are often said to cover forty years. A technical counting shows that it was actually 38+ years, but the Hebrews are known to have used specific numbers for general quantities, and a part of a year at each end would be counted as a whole. Ten could mean "some" while forty could mean "many" or perhaps "a generation." Seven was the number of completion or totality, and twelve sometimes has the same meaning. One thousand means perfection or completeness, sometimes a large quantity, so "ten thousand times ten thousand and thousands of thousands" means simply an enormous multitude. The number 144,000 consists of 12 x 12 x 1,000, and carries the concept of totality and multitude at once. One must therefore be very careful about putting extreme pressure on Hebrew numbers and expecting and requiring the same exact senses as Americans do in the computer age.

---

[7]*The Ancestry of Our English Bible*, 2nd Revised Edition, p. 222.

In Genesis 1 we find lists, such as of astronomical bodies, creatures in the sea, on land, and of plant life. The heavenly bodies such as galaxies, comets, or planets are not mentioned. For all this to make sense, we must understand that the purpose was to express a totality of God's creative activity for the ordinary man's understanding, not to furnish an actual scientific list as a modern auditor would need for an absolute and precise checking.

The 600,000 number of men given for the Exodus escape from Egypt found in Exodus 12:37 would normally require about two million people including the older men, women and children, and this has been considered by critics as an impossible number. Ramm observes that the same Hebrew word for "thousands" may also be translated as "family" or "tent group," and thus there may well have been only about 27,000 total people in the Exodus group, which would be a quite reasonable number.[8]

Since it is impossible to treat here more than just a sample of the detailed difficulties, we cite the readers to the literature where entire volumes are given to explaining these point by point.[9]

Archaeology's Contribution

The results of archaeological studies have been tremendous in confirming the Bible and removing apparent discrepancies. Archaeology is a recent science, and only since about 1940 have we learned its real impact. William F. Albright, for years the world's foremost Biblical archaeologist, stated, "To sum up, we can now treat the Bible from beginning to end as an authentic document of religious history. Innumerable clarifications of the text greatly improve our understanding."[10] G. E. Wright,

---

[8]Bernard Ramm, "Science and Biblical Inerrancy," Journal of the American Scientific Affiliation, V. 21, No. 4, Dec. 1969, pp. 101,2.

[9]Arndt, W., Does the Bible Contradict Itself?, 5th Ed. Rev., St. Louis: Concordia Publishing House, 1957; Haley, John W., Alleged Discrepancies of the Bible, Nashville: B. C. Goodpasture, Reprint, 1951; Torrey, R. A., Difficulties in the Bible, New York: Fleming Revell Co., 1907.

[10]Christian Century, Nov. 19, 1958, p. 1330.

formerly of Harvard Divinity School, defended Nelson Glueck's statement: "It may be categorically stated that no archaeological discovery has ever controverted a Biblical reference," and also Glueck's assertion, "The almost incredibly accurate memory of the Bible and particularly so when it is fortified by archaeological fact."[11]

In summary, therefore, we say the Bible still stands, as it has always stood, against unfair criticism, and it has influenced humanity for good more than anything else in the last two thousand years, even though there have been "apparent discrepancies" all the while.

We would say that if any person should conclude that there are absolute errors in Scripture, and that no answer shall ever be found to explain them, he has by that decision declared himself as having infallible and certain knowledge.

---

[11]*Biblical Archaeologist*, Dec., 1959, p. 101.

CHAPTER 4

INSPIRATION OF THE BIBLE — A PLENARY VIEW

The inspiration of the Scriptures means simply that they are "God-breathed," as the word *theopneustos* (2 Tim. 3:16) says. By this it is understood that God supernaturally controlled the production of the books of the Bible by means of the Holy Spirit's influence upon the writers so that the words of the original manuscripts are exactly what God wanted them to be. The men were so inspired or controlled so that the end product was precisely what was desired, yet it is well-known that the writers of Scriptures used their own vocabularies and their own knowledge of history, geography, and other such matters. These are clearly detectable by students of Greek.

There are many wrong views about what inspiration means or includes. Liberal critics tend to assume that conservative scholars believe in a method of strict "passive dictation," whereby the writer becomes a mere machine, a pen rather than a penman, and makes no contribution of his own of any kind. This is not what is meant by those who hold to a doctrine of verbal inspiration, however. Other false theories of inspiration include: 1) *Natural genius,* as in Shakespeare, but this eliminates the supernatural and in no way assures inerrancy; 2) *Degrees of inspiration,* where it is held that some Scriptures are "More inspired" than others. There are differences in value of certain portions of Scripture, but not in inspiration. All have equal approval of God for the purposes for which they were written; 3) *Inspired Ideas,* where God gave the person an idea and let him write it in his own way. This view would allow more or less error, so that there could be no assurance of infallibility. It insists that the concepts of the men were good, but the mistakes were theirs in putting them into words; thus the Bible is both good and bad at the same time; 4) *Partial inspiration,* where the Bible is inspired in certain portions but not in others. This leaves a problem of deciding which part is dependable and which is not, and ultimately leaves it to the personal preference of the reader; and 5) *Verbal or passive dictation,* where the agent is a mere stenographer, and contributes nothing whatever, as noted above. This is obviously not what happened,

19

but it is not necessary to believe in order for us to have an actual word-certainty.

Plenary inspiration is the name commonly used to indicate the view of a definite and sufficient inspiration to insure that the end product has the precise and exact words, yet without committing oneself to any exact plan of how the Holy Spirit actually functioned in inspiration. It holds that the Bible is inspired so that there is no error in a real sense (though there may be apparent discrepancies), and that the person who depends upon the Bible can do so, because the writings in the original manuscripts were written accurately and they say exactly what God wanted said. In this way plenary inspiration is "verbal" in its end results, though it is not what is called "passive dictation." As to method, the Holy Spirit did what ever was necessary to have absolute control of the end product, though He may well have used different methods for different portions of Scripture, and in different contextual situations. Indeed, some portions may well be "passive dictation" e.g.:

> 2 Sam. 23:2 - The Spirit of the Lord speaks by me, his word is upon my tongue.

> 2 Peter 1:21 - . . . no prophecy ever came by the impulse of man, but men moved by the Holy Spirit spoke from God.

while at other times we may well have allowed a strong use of the previous knowledge of the human author, as in the different vocabularies used in the several books. This "flexible" view accommodates all of the known facts about the Biblical text, yet it allows a faith that can be confident of divine control, so that one can believe that when he rightly interprets a passage he is getting God's exact will on the point.

The Bible may be looked at as a *record* of God's revelation, but in fact and in truth it *is itself* revelation. When a man learns the Bible's teachings, he personally is receiving revelation at that time.

Inspiration of the Bible includes the concept of revelation, but it also includes the selection: of subject matter, of existing documents, records, historical matters to be used, and the accurate recording of statements, teaching and similar matters.

It goes all the way to the correct wording, but this in no wise destroys the individuality of the writer, nor does it exclude the need for him to study and do research and careful thinking in a human way.

Plenary inspiration is a view that is concerned with the *extent* of inspiration and with the *results,* but does not require that one know the mode of exactly how it was accomplished. It is concerned with the "What," but not the "How." All parts of the Bible are equally inspired, but all are not equally important and many have different significance to different individuals in different situations.

Inspired men were inspired for the writing of Scripture, and some of them as oral teachers of God's word. No one today is inspired in this sense. No more Bibles are being written, or shall be.

CHAPTER 5

THE COLLECTION OF THE BOOKS OF THE BIBLE

A logical question that arises as we consider the history of the Bible is, "Do we have the right books in the Bible?" This question presupposes that there should be a Bible in the first place, and that the historical process by which the books were selected is knowable, and indeed, that errors might have been made in the selection.

The canonicity (the test of selection) of any book of Scripture is dependent upon its being considered as inspired and thus expressly given by God for the guidance of men. An important consideration is the fact that some books, written earlier, were considered and used as Scripture before others were written. So, well-known books of Scriture existed before there was the complete Bible. Actually each Testament, Old and New, grew silently and imperceptibly until it reached completion. Acceptance by the people of God was a part in the process of "official" canonization, and each writing therefore earned its own way. Never did a group of men sit down at a council table and *make* a book canonical. Councils only served to ratify those writings which had already demonstrated themselves and had been commonly accepted as having the qualities of Scripture.

The Old Testament

There are numerous witnesses or sources which testify to the Old Testament's books as rightly belonging to the category of God's word. The book itself points out that the Ten Commandments were placed in the ark (Ex. 31:8); the "Book of the Law" was to be kept beside the ark (Deut. 31:24-26); was to be read publicly every seven years (Deut. 31:10-13); was to be meditated upon and taught by Joshua (Josh. 1:7, 8), and was to control future kings of Israel (Deut. 17:18-20). The *"Law"* is referred to about 75 times in the historical books, and it was to serve as the basis for the rebuilding of the Jewish nation and worship program after the Babylonian captivity.

The *prophets* were acknowledged as Jehovah's spokesmen for their day, speaking with a "thus said the Lord." The prophetical writings are called "Scripture" 43 times in the New Testament, while the *"writings"* (the other Old Testament books) are called Scripture 37 times in the New Testament.

Several Old Testament books were written in the period immediately following the Babylonian captivity, coming to a close probably about 432 B.C. The canon obviously was not "closed" until then, but it was generally understood among the Jews that there was no prophet among the people between this time and the time of the New Testament. Josephus, a Jewish historian of the first century A.D. says this specifically:

> For we have not an innumerable multitude of books amongst us, disagreeing from and contradicting one another (as the Greeks have), but only 22 books, which contain the record of all time; which are justly believed to be divine. And of these, 5 are books of Moses, which contain the laws and traditions from the origin of mankind till his (Moses') death. This interval of time is a little short of 3,000 years. But as to the time from the death of Moses till the reign of Artaxerxes, king of Persia, who reigned after Xerxes, the prophets who were after Moses wrote down what was done in their time in 13 books. The remaining 4 books contain hymns to God and precepts for the conduct of human life. It is true, our history has been written since Artaxerxes very particularly, but has not been esteemed of like authority with the former by our forefathers, because there has not been an exact succession of prophets since that time. And how firmly we have given credit to those books of our own nation, is evident by what we do; for, during so many ages as have already passed, no one has been so bold as either to add anything to them, to take anything from them, or to make any change in them; but it becomes natural to all Jews, immediately and from their very birth, to esteem those books to contain divine doctrines, and to persist in them, and, if occasion be, willingly to die for them.
>
> —Contra Apionem 1:8

Josephus thus observes that the succession of prophets had ceased between the Testaments, and that the writing of the Old Testament dated between Moses and the time of Artaxerxes, who reigned in 424 B.C. Likely, then, the Old Testament canon was complete by the days of Ezra and Nehemiah, and they might well have had a part in its final collection.

Jewish Old Testament is and always has been identical with our 39-book Old Testament. IV Esdras, written about 90 A.D., lists 24 books — five of Law, eight of prophets, and eleven of writings. The eight prophets would include both "former" and "latter," with the twelve minor prophets counted as one book as was customary to the Jews. Josephus' number of 22 books, the number of letters in the Hebrew alphabet, probably adds Ruth to Judges and Lamentations to Jeremiah, to equal the number of twenty-four.

The *Septuagint,* indicated by scholars as the "LXX," is the Greek language Old Testament which was translated in the third century B.C. It is a strong witness to the fact of there being a canon of Holy Scripture at that time, though it does not give a precise indication of which books. Our oldest manuscripts of the LXX vary as to books included, but they are all at least 500 years younger than the original translation, and they were produced outside of Palestine, probably in Alexandria.

Other witnesses to the Old Testament canon include Ecclesiasticus, a Jewish apocryphal wisdom book written about 200 B.C., and which catalogues all the Old Testament heroes all the way from Adam to Nehemiah, who was chronologically last. It says that all wisdom is to be derived from a study of the Law. The Prologue to Ecclesiasticus was written in 132 B.C. by a grandson of the author of the original work and mentions the threefold division of the Old Testament books into Law, Prophets and Writings. Both First and Second Maccabees, written in the second century B.C., show an awareness of the Old Testament writings, and Philo of Alexandria, a Jewish philosopher of the first century A.D. quoted the canonical books but not the apocryphal ones. He revered the Law of Moses. Eusebius reports that of it Philo said, "They have not changed so much as a single word in them. They would rather die a thousand deaths than detract anything from these laws and statutes."[12]

---

[12]Quoted by George L. Robinson in the *New International Standard Bible Encyclopedia,* 1939 Ed., Vol. I, p. 558b, Grand Rapids: Wm. B. Eerdmans Pub. Co.

The New Testament further witnesses to the Old Testament by quoting every book of it except Esther, Ecclesiastes and the Song of Solomon (this accepts the regular counting of the twelve minor prophets as one book). It quotes no apocryphal book (seven additional books which are included in the Roman Catholic Bible), but it quotes the canonical ones and alludes to them specifically as many as a thousand or more times, calling them "Scripture," and quoting, "It is written," and in many cases mentioning the name of the person quoted.

The Apocrypha

The Catholic Old Testament has seven books and portions of two others that are not in the Protestant or Jewish Old Testament lists. These books, called the Aprocrypha ("hidden"), were not adopted by the Catholics until 1562 A.D., after they were under pressure from Protestantism. No one of these books was ever in any Jewish Bible; they are not quoted in the New Testament; they were written outside Palestine in the period between the Testaments when there was "no prophet" among the Jews; they were rejected by Josephus, Philo, the Council of Jamnia (90 A.D.), by Origen, and by practically all Scripture lists of the first four centuries A.D. Also Jerome, the translator of the Vulgate, the official Catholic Bible, was out-spoken against them. They have errors and self-contradictions. They teach salvation by works, magical incantations, and approve lying, suicide, assassination, and prayers for the dead. They include legendary materials and other absurdities. It is true that Augustine accepted some of them in a secondary sense, but he would not allow doctrine to be proved by them. Pope Clement VII (1378-94 A.D.), less than two centuries before they were placed into the canon, rejected them "as confirming those things which are of faith," yet he did accept them as helpful "for edification."

The New Testament

Since God's people had a book of Scripture in the Old Testament period, it is quite logical and to be expected that there should be a New Testament as the Christian book revealing God's authoritative will. The church began without its own *book,* though it did not begin without the word of God, since the inspired gospel was preached orally from Pentecost day right on through to the time of writing of the New Testament books which were written between about 50 A.D. and 100 A.D., though they did not circulate together as one volume until later. Each writing was considered as inspired and authoritative from its origin, however. Most of them were written by men who were known to be inspired and authoritative in their oral communications, so it was only natural that their writings would automatically be accepted as inspired.

The process of canonization was gradual and silent, though we have some early indications of recognition. Paul's books, completed in the 60's, are believed by scholars to have been circulating together by about 90 A.D.[13] while the four gospels were accepted as circulating together by about 120 A.D.[14] The New Testament as a book was translated into Old Latin and Syriac within the second century, A.D., and into about a dozen different foreign languages by the third century.[15] This was not customarily done unless books were deemed of great value (the Old Testament's translation into Greek is the first instance ever known of the translation of a book from one language into another). The slowness of final canonization may because some books are less central in their message than others, and probably these were slower in becoming fully disseminated among the people. The six slowest books to receive acceptance were James, 2 Peter, 2 and 3 John, Jude and Revelation. They are generally less used by Christians of today, and this may explain the point. Books of the New Testament were profusely quoted by the church fathers and other early Christian writers, beginning with 1 Clement in 95 A.D. The term "New Testament," used outside of the book itself, is first found in an 192 A.D.[16] writing, but is

---

[13]E. J. Goodspeed, *History of Early Christian Literature*, Chicago: University of Chicago Press, 1942, p. 10.
[14]Ibid., p. 61.
[15]B.M. Metzger, "Versions, Ancient," in *Interpreters Bible Dictionary*, Vol. IV, p. 749f.
[16]S. Riggs, in *New International Standard Bible Encyclopedia*, 1939 Ed., Grand Rapids: Wm. B. Eerdmans, Vol. I, p. 565.

found frequently thereafter. One "church father," Origen, quoted the New Testament 17,922 times in his known writings, and seven men between 150 A.D. and 325 A.D. have left us 36,289 quotations of it in their known writings.[17]

Both Catholics and Protestants accept the 27-book New Testament without variation.

---

[17]H. S. Miller, *General Biblical Introduction*, 4th Edition, Houghton, N.Y.: Word Bearer Press, 1944, p. 259.

CHAPTER 6

THE WORDING OF THE BIBLE, FROM THE FIRST MANUSCRIPTS TO TODAY

A question that some people of today ask is, How can we be sure that we have the same wording in the Bible of today that was in the original manuscripts? What assurance is there that there has not been a large body of errors that have crept in during the period that the book has been in existence, with all its copying? The question is made even more challenging when we sometimes read articles in popular magazines that are intended to sound sensational, implying that there are so many erros or variations between the manuscripts of Scripture that we must despair of ever knowing what was originally written. Estimates of "errors" in the New Testament have been said to run from 50,000 to 200,000, even though the entire book has only about 6,000 verses and approximately 180,000 words. We would note that the great majority of variants are trivial, involving only matters of spelling, word order, syntactical variants of the same word, and errors of the copyist that are clearly recognizable as such.

But the question still remains — Are there any real variations that involve errors in substance, so that we cannot know God's will for sure? Are there serious mistakes that make valid faith impossible?

First, we should observe that the *copying* of the Scriptures was not inspired or under supernatural control. No one believes that copyists were inspired. This is why all the copyists were subject to making normal human mistakes. Only the original manuscripts were inspired, and the concept of infallibility and inerrancy therefore apply only to them. If this were not true, any copyist of today would have to become inspired the moment he chose to copy a portion of Scripture. This obviously is non-sensical. Although the Holy Spirit indwells Christians in a meaningful way today, no one considers that he does so in the sense of inspiring the writing of Scripture. No new Bibles or portions of Scripture are being written today!

At this point we probably should note that present-day

versions of the Scriptures need not be inspired and infallible for us to assuredly know God's will. The science of Textual Criticism is able to compare manuscripts and evaluate them as to their variations, and by this study it does assure us adequately as to the correct original reading. No major doctrine or important teaching is at stake among the known variants, and we can determine the original wording through Textual Criticism to a degree that puts any major concern beyond question, and this is true even for critical scholars. We have what was in the original manuscripts, for all practical needs and purposes. One reason for this assurance is that today we have about 5,000 hand-written New Testament manuscripts, varying from each other, in the different libraries of the world, but only one hundred or so of other major human writings, such as the works of Homer. To compare this number of witnesses is to arrive at assurance.

Textual Variants

There are, to be sure, numerous variants in the several extant New Testament manuscripts. Their existence is no cause for alarm, however, as noted above. F. C. Grant, a member of the Committee for the Revised Standard Version of the New Testament, has said, ". . . no doctrine of the Christian faith has been affected by the revision for the simple reason that out of the thousands of variant readings in the manuscripts, none has turned up thus far that requires a revision of Christian doctrine."[18] Each of the variants involves only a small amount of text. There are only two "large" variants in the entire 6,000 verse New Testament, each of twelve verses.[19] There are several that involve as much as one verse, but the rest are only of a phrase or a word, or a variation within the word such as its spelling or ending for syntax purposes.

Although the several manuscripts extant today have these variations between themselves, this is no more than we would

---

[18]F. C. Grant in *An Introduction to the Revised Standard Version of the New Testament,* Luther A. Weigle, Editor. International Council of Religious Education, 1946, p. 42.

[19]Mark 16:9-20 and John 7:53-8:11.

normally expect of unaided human scribes. (Human beings still need to buy pencils with erasers on them.) The singular thing about the New Testament variants is that they are all of fringe significance, with no distinctive doctrine of any one church group being dependent upon how they read. The twelve-verse variation which is the story of the adulterous woman (John 7:53-8:11) has comparatively weak evidence in the major manuscripts for this passage, but there is no important doctrine at stake or which is not covered clearly elsewhere. The other "long" passage is the twelve-verse ending of Mark's gospel (16:9-20). Our two "best" manuscripts (4th Century A.D.) do not have this reading, but several good manuscripts do. It is quoted within the second century by Irenaeus, and it is included in many of the ancient versions into languages other than Greek, including the Old Latin and Syriac which date well within the second century, A.D.

English Versions

Comment should no doubt be made with respect to the numerous English versions of the New Testament that now confront the Bible reader. For many years the King James version was the only contender of note and it dominated the scene for almost 300 years. In general it was a good version and it served to set standards for the English language. In fact, it helped greatly in aiding English to become what may some day prove to be the dominant language of the world. The King James was quite limited by not having an adequate number of good manuscripts on which to depend, and also the changes in word meanings over the years have contributed to its becoming outdated in many respects, although it is still a favorite of many and its beauty of expression will probably never be excelled.

We should realize that all translating of the original manuscripts of the Bible is uninspired, and is therefore subject to human error. For this reason dependable translations should not be the work of one man, but rather should be the work of large committees, and normally representing scholars of various faiths. In this way they can check on each other and prevent distorted readings which might tend to favor one theology or another. Since languages themselves grow and change, it is imperative that new translations be made from time to time to keep the meanings the same for current readers as they were for the original readers. We should also realize that we are fortunate today to have so many manuscripts from which to draw evidence, and so many qualified scholars in practically all faiths who can handle the materials in appropriate scholarly fashion. There is every good reason to believe that we have the Bible today in essentially the same wording as the original manuscripts, and that we therefore need have no doubt about God's word to us. The many good commentaries and numerous other study helps (such as no *human* writing has ever enjoyed) make it possible for today's student, more so than in any other age, to have a certainty that God's revelation is his. The big need, of course, is for men to seriously study it as the word of God and to live out its teachings in their lives.

As to the text of the Old Testament, the Jews were always careful about textual matters in their copying. For instance, it was customary in hand-copying the Scriptures, for them to destroy a page entirely and start all over if they made an error on the last line. When a manuscript wore out from handling, they buried it with appropriate ceremonies, perhaps in pottery jars in caves similar to the way the Dead Sea Scrolls were deposited (See Jeremiah 32:14).

Because of the carefulness of Jewish scribes, and also probably because old manuscripts were carefully disposed of, variants are much fewer between the known manuscripts of the Old Testament than of the New. After printing was learned variants in both Testaments are few and are usually deliberate, since printed copies are alike. This new invention occurred about the middle of the 15th century A.D. In modern times there are many more scholars and a greater study of textual problems, and the consensus is that there is no serious doubt about anything of great importance in either Testament. We have a proliferation of new English translations, and although paraphrases and one-man translations are highly suspect there is no reason to question the major translations as being basically true to the original autographs — sufficiently so that one need not be concerned about any major or even serious errors. If one of them should have an error the others will usually agree in making the correction.

EXTERNAL EVIDENCES

CHAPTER 7

THE IMPACT OF ARCHAEOLOGY
OF BIBLICAL FAITH

Christianity will never be removed from the realm of faith by "proving" its basic tenets to be final, absolute truth, but it need not be. It was meant for man to "walk by faith, and not by sight" (2 Cor. 5:7). All people live by a faith of some sort, even the atheists and skeptics. No man can scientifically prove any truth in the realm of spiritual realities, so the atheist can no more prove his position than can the theist.

Biblical Archaeology aids faith in that it is able to confirm facts upon which faith is based, but of course it is not able to fully and finally "prove" that biblical faith is the right faith. It also gives light upon interpretative problems and it corrects had theories that men may have about the Bible. Faith is not dependent upon Archaeology, since men had faith before the science of Archaeology was ever contemplated.

Archaeology is a comparatively recent contributor to biblical knowledge since the most of its great conclusions were determined after about 1935. The determination of strata between the ancient cities in a mound, and the learning of the dates for the various types of pottery found in the strata facilitated the dating process for the several occupations of each mound. The accumulation, then, of all the knowable facts from several sources has allowed the reconstruction of life patterns for the different periods.

General Confirmations

Most of the biblical sites have been located, including about 44 or 45 of the 48 Levitical Cities. The Conquest of Canaan by the Israelites is confirmed, in that the order of cities taken fits in with the terrain of the hills, the evidence of violent destruction at Bethel, Lachish and Debir at least approximate the right dates, and during this same period new towns began to dot the hill country, clearly distinct from the Canaanite towns and the Philistine towns that were there previously. The Exodus from Egypt is recognized as an unquestioned reality and the Tell-el

Amarna letters may be testimony to the entrance of the Israelites into Canaan.

Critical scholars once had firmly concluded that Moses could not have written the first five books of the Old Testament, since they were written in Semitic alphabetic language and it was thought that no such writing existed in Moses' day. In 1931, however, a library of clay tablets was unearthed at Ras Shamra, or Ugarit, which dated well before Moses and which has an abundance of materials in definite Semitic alphabetic language. At Ebla in Northern Palestine discoveries have recently been made that reflect the civilization in that area some 400-700 years before Abraham's day, and other facts have been found that clearly mark him as belonging to the day (about 1,900 B.C.) to which the Bible assigns him. The Mitannians, the Horites, the Amorites and the Hittites have all been located and identified, whereas they formerly were mere names. As Wm. F. Albright says,

> Abraham, Isaac and Jacob no longer seem isolated figures, much less reflections of later Israelite history; they now appear as true children of their age, bearing the same names, moving about over the same territory, visiting the same towns, practicing the same customs as their contemporaries. In other words, the patriarchal narratives have a historical nucleus throughout.[20]

Other finds, to name only a few of the many that confirm biblical history, are:

- The Ras Shamra texts mention the same deities of the Canaanites that the Old Testament does.

- There are many parallel words, phrases and ideas that are contemporary with the Old Testament.

- The poetry in the Ras Shamra materials is similar to that of Hebrew — as lines, forms, parallelism, etc.

---

[20]Albright, Wm. F., *The Archaeology of Palestine,* Baltimore: Penguin Books, Ltd., 1960 Reprint, p. 236.

- The *names* found in the patriarchal narratives fit into the list of those belonging to the period from 2,000 to 1,500 B.C., but not into a later period.

Again as Albright mentions,

The Biblical historical data are accurate to an extent far surpassing the ideas of many modern critical students, who have constantly tended to err on the side of hypercriticism.[21]

"Light" furnished by Archaeology for interpretation of otherwise hazy passages could include the following:

- An inscription found at Delphi on the "mainland" of Greece gives us a firm date for Paul's arraignment before Gallio (see Acts 18:12-17), and from this we can arrive at our firmest date for the writing of a New Testament book, that of the First Thessalonian letter, about 50 A.D.

- The term "shambles" implying a "meat market" (1 Cor. 10:25), comes from the Greek word *makkellon,* and may get meaning from the fact that underground tunnels bearing cold water from mountain springs ran underneath and at the back of a series of shops along the Lechaeum road at Corinth. This meat, slaughtered in a pagan festival, could after covering be submerged into the cold water which to some degree could serve as a sort of refrigerant for a time.

- The matter of "consulting the oracle" for information from a pagan deity is illuminated by the finding of an oracular shrine in the midst of the public marketplace in Corinth. It was a little private shrine room with a fountain bubbling up in its center. Digging has shown that a tunnel carried the overflow water away, but another tunnel, large enough for a man to crawl up in, was parallel to it. At the fountain, a megaphone-type hole went from this latter tunnel into the fountain. A pagan priest could then crawl into the tunnel at stated

---

times and could actually hear and answer questions from the worshipper, who assumed that the god was replying to him. A warning sign to stay away from the area near the tunnel entrance some distance away confirms this practice. When we read about the *oracles of God* in scripture, we thus know that the implication for those readers, therefore, is that the scriptures are intended as God's specific message to us.

For historical confirmations in general we note that a papyrus document has been found that is datable for each year in the first century, A.D., and that writings from the thousands of clay tablets found at Ras Shamra, Nuzi, Mari, Chagar-Bazar and Ebla furnish all manner of light on the culture and life of those who lived in the days recorded in the Old Testament, from before Abraham on down.

On the question of learning about the text and writing of the New Testament, archaeology has discovered the Beatty papyri, a large portion of the New Testament dating from about 200 A.D.; the John Rylands fragment, a small portion of the Gospel of John dating about 140 A.D.; the Nash papyrus; the Dead Sea Scrolls; numerous Gnostic manuscripts, and several other important witnesses. For the Old Testament there is the Gezer inscription (900 B.C.); the Mesha stone (835); the Siloam inscription (722); the Lachish letters (589 — Jeremiah's time); the Samaritan Ostraca (Hosea's time). With all this information scholars can reconstruct the script and spelling of both the Hebrew and Greek Old Testaments, and thus a revision of Lexicons, Grammars and Commentaries was called for by this abundance of new data. Rare and archaic words from Canaanite and Mesopotamian texts have also come to light in great quantity.

Summary

For a summary of the impact of archaeology on the credibility of the Bible, we quote some additional observations from the pen of W. F. Albright, who was recognized during his day by all theological schools as the best informed and most authoritative of all biblical archaeologists:

While the writer has gradually changed from the extreme radicalism of 1919 to a standpoint which can neither be called conservative nor radical in the usual sense of the terms . . .[22]

Archaeological discovery has been largely responsible for the recent revival of interest in Biblical theology . . . It becomes clearer each day that this rediscovery of the Bible often leads to a new evaluation of Biblical faith, which strikingly resembles the orthodoxy of an earlier day. Neither an academic scholasticism nor an irresponsible neo-orthodoxy must be allowed to divert our eyes from the living faith of the Bible.[23]

The problems of historical and literary criticism which disturbed our fathers when freed rudely from certain pre-conceived ideas to which they had become attached, no longer disturb a generation of Biblical scholars who are discovering that they must retrace their steps toward a rational conservatism. We no longer trouble ourselves with attempts to "harmonize" religion and science, or to "prove" the Bible. The Bible can stand by itself; it has suffered more from its well-intentioned friends than from its honest foes. As research and discovery continue it will become greater and greater in the widening perspective which they will give to our children.[24]

In any case the Bible towers in content about all earlier religious literature; and it towers just as impressively over all subsequent literature in the direct simplicity of its message and the catholicity of its appeal to men of all lands and times.[25]

and finally,

To all who believe in the eternal value of the Old and New Testaments it is clear that God has been preparing a way for a revival of basic Christianity through enlightened faith in His word. It is no accident that archaeology and its ancillary disciplines have revolutionized our historical approach to the Bible.[26]

---

[22]*Bulletin American Schools of Oriental Research*, #51, September 1933, pp. 5, 6.
[23]*Religion in Life*, Autumn, 1952, p. 550.
[24]Appendix to *Young's Analytical Concordance*, p. 51.
[25]*Christian Century*, Nov. 19, 1958, p. 1330.
[26]Ibid, p. 1331.

CHAPTER 8

THE FACT OF THE CHURCH —
ITS GENIUS, EXPANSION AND HISTORY

The existence of the church established by Jesus (cf. Matt. 16:18f) and now existing for two thousand years is a positive testimony to the Bible as God's message to man. The church had its beginning on Pentecost day following the resurrection of Jesus (see Acts 2), and it captured the imagination and faith of peoples from all over the eastern Mediterranean world in a short time. It grew and expanded until it dominated the Roman empire by 325 A.D., with the emperor Constantine even declaring Sunday to be a legal holiday. He also was instrumental in taking over some pagan temples and making them into Christian places of worship; he paid for several major copies of the scriptures to be produced on sheepskin with tax monies; and he declared that numerous advantages and benefits should be granted to those who preached the word and ministered in the faith.

There is a certain genius to the gospel appeal in that it changes the hearts of individuals for good (see Phil. 2:1-11). Repentance of sins and a determination to live in harmony with God's teachings makes men different, so much so that real Christian living is noticeable in any culture. It was noticeable in the culture of first century Palestine and the eastern Mediterranean area and this factor made many wish to investigate the new religion and turn to it. It is a different religion from any other known. Although Judaism was the biblical religion of Old Testament times, thus divinely approved for the period, Christianity is quite different from Judaism, as it is from other religions.

Christianity is a personal relationship, between the human adherent and the person of Jesus Christ. It calls for the recognition of a crucified Jew as very God, but in this recognition and confession, one makes a commitment that is a complete renunciation of self and a sincere promise to live a yielded life. It is the response which puts one, in faith, into a right relationship with the Creator God and his universe. It is the life, when rightly understood, which all men are really looking for. It has clear answers for questions about the meaning of life. So, throughout the ages it has proved to be a faith that men have been willing to die for, and also to live for. It has a spiritual power that is undeniable.

The church as a kingdom made up of baptized believers has corporate responsibilities — of preaching the gospel and of carrying on the work of the Lord in every age. It is the fellowship of the saints, and where its doctrines have not become distorted, it has proved to be a true witness to God's will and his way. Its existence through the centuries and its influence in the world in spite of distortions are demonstrations to the world of the integrity of the scriptural teachings and of the power of the word of God.

As a fact of history, the church cannot be explained without its supernatural origins and its supernaturally inspired teachings found in the New Testament. It is these *extras,* which unaided man could not produce, that give it its real genius and its appeal to all mankind when it is taught and explained to them. This is why the gospel is to be "preached to all nations."

The Fact of the Bible

The existence and origin of the Bible itself also calls for an acceptance of supernatural power. The Old Testament was written by about thirty or so men over a period of about a thousand years. For about four hundred years after the Old Testament was completed, no scripture was written (see the Josephus quotation in Chapter V above), and then in 50 A.D., inspiration again became operative and during the last half of the first century A.D. twenty-seven new books were written which dove-tail exactly with the Old Testament, in fulfillment of its prophecies and in presenting the new Christian religion, which is the zenith and the *summum-bonum* of God's "plan of redemption" which he purposed from the beginning.[27] Christianity is the "new Israel" and when the Law of Moses was "taken out of the way and nailed to the cross" (see Col. 2:14),

---

[27]See 1 Peter 1:20 and Revelation 13:8 (note).

the new faith with its new atonement, the blood of Christ, became operative. Thus, we can see a historical fulfillment documented today in the light of the two Testaments.

The abundance of manuscript evidence concerning the biblical books from the earliest days proclaim empirically that people considered these writings of the inspired men to be God's word, right from the time they were written. Their spiritual power is acknowledged even by critical scholars to be superior to the non-canonical writings. The fact that the twenty-seven books of our New Testament earned their own way into the new canon, and that serious scholarship of today would not choose to add any other writings, is adequate reason to believe in their spiritual superiority. Never man spake like Jesus, and never men wrote like the biblical writers.

The existence of the church and the Bible and the faith of the early Christians — that Jesus was the Christ the Son of God — have actually caused a revolution in western culture and western thought. America was founded in the thought matrix of the western civilization of Europe, which had in turn derived its basic world view from Christian teachings. The progress of man in his scientific and intellectual achievements has prospered under the aegis of Christianity, since, above all, Christianity accepts the order and the uniformity in nature. Since man was to dominate his world (Gen. 1:28), scientific investigation and discovery brings no fears for faith.

A further impact of the Bible upon western civilization is to be noted in our basic world-view concerning the value of a man — of human life and of the value of one human soul, which Jesus said is worth more than all the world (Matt. 16:26). When our news commentators of today describe an accident or a calamity, the primary concern is danger to the human life, not the loss of dollars and cents. This says much about the influence of Christian ideas in our culture.

Baptism and the Lord's Supper

The practice of Christian immersion, or baptism, as an initiating ceremony into the benefits of Christianity has been practiced from Pentecost day until now, and this fact is abundantly documented throughout all ages of church history. Again, the very interesting observance of the Lord's Supper each Lord's day from the beginnings of the Christian movement until now, with each Christian "remembering" the Lord's death by partaking of the loaf and the fruit of the vine — an also fully documentable historical fact — is strong witness to the continuing power of the Christian movement and of the teachings of Christ right from the start of Christian history.

The Resurrection and the Resurrection Faith

Among the major problems that critics who deny the Bible as being the inspired word of God have to face is the question of the resurrection of Jesus Christ. From the standpoint of the scientist who assumes that natural law is all there is, the resurrection is impossible, since it never happens today, and it would be a violation of natural law as we know it. (Of course evolutionists believe that life on earth *first began* as a violation of natural law — since the laws of nature insist that "life comes only from life," and therefore until life first existed, other life forms could not be so generated.)

The supernatural origin of our universe must be recognized as a logical possibility. There is no way to prove that it originated supernaturally or only naturally — either view is only a faith, but each is as logically possible as the other. The atheist who says that there is no God, would have to be omniscient for the statement to mean anything, because if there were one thing he did not know, it might be that God exists. So we are forced to accept the possibility of the supernatural origin of the universe and of man, and in such a case, the resurrection of Christ from the dead is logically possible if the Creator God chose to cause it as an integral factor in his plan of redemption for man.

Arguments in favor of a literal resurrection include the eye-witnesses who knew the Lord before and after his death on the cross. These were not gullible people (see John 20:24, 25). The fact of his death was well-known and he appeared after the resurrection to disciples on a dozen different occasions — and to above 500 people in one assembly. Had the story been untrue it could have easily been proved wrong in his own day, as his enemies would have done (cf. Matt. 27:62-65). There were also people who were not disciples who knew of the mighty works of Jesus and of his teaching and of the preaching about him after the church began on Pentecost day. Jesus was only thirty-three years old at his death and some of his close disciples lived until in the 90's A.D., while no doubt many non-Christian eyewitnesses lived throughout his personal ministry and well on into the period of the spread of Christianity and knew of the preaching of a literal resurrection, so there was ample opportunity for refutation if it had been possible.

The enemies of the resurrection in the earliest days were faced with an empty tomb, which has not yet been explained. In view of the resurrection the third day, it could have been contradicted by producing the corpse, and they had concern that the prophecy of the resurrection not be fulfilled.

The resurrection faith of the disciples after the event would be very difficult to justify, since before his death they despaired and thought it was all over. Even Thomas had to put his hand into the nail prints before he could accept the resurrection as a fact. But afterward they stood before kings and other men of importance and declared their faith, at their peril. Many Christians were called upon to die for their faith.

INTERNAL EVIDENCES

CHAPTER 9

FULFILLED PROPHECY

Prophecy and its later fulfillment in detail has always been a real problem to those who were skeptical about supernatural influence in the Bible. Attention was called to fulfilled prophecies by defenders of inspiration in the second century, A.D., in answering the attacks of Porphyry and Celsus. Thus prophecy and fulfillment has been for the entire two thousand years of church history a viable defense of Christian faith, and it has never yet been refuted.

Real prediction demonstrates the supernatural, since ordinary man cannot know in detail even one hour in advance of an event. For this reason, scholars who have a presupposition against supernaturalism in the production of the Bible attempt to date prophetical statements late, so that they can be counted as history rather than as a prediction. (It could well be that some things can be predicted, as an educated guess, if factors seem to be already coming together in favor of a certain conclusion, like predicting who will win an election two days before election day.) Nahum's prediction about Nineveh, which fell in 612 B.C., is thus dated by Liberal scholars at 614 B.C. The historical "build-up" was already present, but Liberals do not accept the earlier date generally held by conservatives because a date that early would require a supernatural prediction. Likewise, they date Isaiah, chapters 40-66, later than Isaiah's own lifetime because it mentions the name of Cyrus, king of Persia, who lived about 160 years later than Isaiah. It would have required supernatural power to make this prediction of a king's name that length of time before he became king. Again Isaiah, chapter 53, has about seventeen separate predictions about the person and activities of Jesus Christ, all in one twelve-verse chapter. This is the most "Messianic" passage in the Old Testament, and it is a real thorn-in-the-flesh for naturalistic scholarship, for the simple reason that it convinces the ordinary reader that inspiration is at work here. No one man could order his life to fulfill all these details, if he had only natural abilities! An experienced personal-worker friend of this writer has declared that in his judgment "fulfilled prophecies" furnish the most convincing arguments to unbelievers who turn to accept the word. A former student of mine found 94 specific Messianic prophecies in the Old Testament that had specific New Testament fulfillments. *Nestle's Greek Testament* lists in its appendix more than one thousand passages in the Old Testament quoted or definitely alluded to in the New Testament, although not all of these are strict prophecies.

As stated earlier, the tendency of Liberalism is to date the prophecy passages late, even after the event, if possible, so that they would have been written as a history of the actual event rather than as a prediction. As to Isaiah 53 this passage had to be written more than 500 years before Jesus, so one skeptic has said, "The faith of the prophet was historically realized," which is an admission that Jesus fulfilled these details in his life and person, but thus claiming that it was a "mere coincidence." Another reply, also given personally in this writer's hearing by a recognized professor, was that "we just don't know" who "the Isaiah author" was talking about, which in modern parlance is a "cop-out." A third reaction to Isaiah from a liberal author who wrote the Isaiah material in the *Abingdon Commentary,* published by a "Liberal" press (p. 665) reads:

> Yet — It may relieve the air of that electricity, which is so apt to charge it at the discussion of so classic a passage as this, and secure as calm weather in which to examine exegetical details, if we at once assert, what none but prejudiced Jews have ever denied, that this great prophecy, known as the 53rd of Isaiah, was fulfilled in One Person, Jesus of Nazareth, and achieved in all its details by Him alone."

For this to come from a liberal scholar in a strongly liberal publication, is quite an admission, and must reflect genuine honesty.

Types and Antitypes

A "type" is a word, a person, or an event that has within itself a similarity to its *antitype,* and when the similarity is seen, they become prophecy and fulfillment. The word *type* has the same meaning as the printer's type, since it bears a discernible likeness to the later printed word. The type always precedes the antitype in time, and really exists only for its relation to the antitype, which comes later and is the really important thing in the whole relationship. There are types of persons, things, institutions, events and places. We illustrate:

Persons — Adam, Moses, Aaron and Melchizedek are all types of Christ. (Adam as the physical head of the human race, Moses as Law-giver, Aaron as High Priest, and Melchizedek as an Independent priest.)

Things — Lambs, the sacrificial altar, the Laver, and other items of furniture in the Tabernacle are all typical of spiritual realities of the Christian age.

Institutions — The Sabbath, The Law, and Mount Sinai have their later counterparts.

Events — Egypt, the Red Sea Crossing, the Wilderness life, the Crossing of the Jordan, and life in the land of Canaan all are clearly typical of bondage in sin, of baptism as deliverance, of the Christian life and of heaven, respectively.

Places — The tabernacle and temple are typical of the the church and its worship today.

Specific Prophecies

As indicated above, there is a multitude of prophecies, the most of which are clear enough to give positive testimony to the fact that ordinary natural abilities of man are not adequate to have produced them. For illustrative purposes we list below several of the key "Messianic" prophecies, and, as these together speak of the person and nature of the Messiah when he shall come, they present a powerful witness:

1. He would be the seed of the woman: Gen. 3:15/Matt. 1:18; Gal. 4:4.

2. He would be of the seed of Abraham: Gen. 12:3/Gal. 3:16.

3. He would be of the tribe of Judah: Gen. 49:10/Heb. 7:14.

4. He would be of the seed of David: Psalms 132:11; Jer. 23:5/Acts 20:30, 31; Rom. 1:3.

5. The time of His coming: Dan. 2:44; Joel 2:28, 29/Luke 2:1; Acts 2:16ff.

6. He would be born of a virgin and be named Immanuel: Isaiah 7:14/Matt. 1:20-23.

7. He would be born in Bethlehem: Micah 5:2/Matt. 2:1, 4-6.

8. He would be introduced by John the Baptist: Isaiah 40:3; Mal. 3:1/Matt. 3:1-3; Luke 3:5.

9. He would be a prophet like unto Moses: Deut. 18:15f/Acts 3:20-22.

10. He would be meek, and without ostentation: Isaiah 42:1, 2/Matt. 12:15-21.

11. He would be without guile: Isaiah 53:9/1 Peter 2:21, 22.

12. He would be lowly and ride upon the colt of an ass: Zech. 9:9, 10/John 12:12.

13. He would work miracles: Isaiah 35:5, 6/Matt. 11:4, 5.

14. He would be betrayed by a friend: Psalm 41:9/John 13:18-21.

15. He would be sold for 30 pieces of silver, which would be used to buy a potter's field: Zech. 11:12, 13/Matt. 26:15; 27:5-7.

16. He would be patient and silent in his sufferings: Isaiah 53:7/Matt. 27:12-14.

17. He would be scourged and spit upon: Isaiah 50:6/Matt. 26:67; 27:26.

18. He would suffer, to bear our sins: Isaiah 53:4-6/Matt. 26:28, 38. (This one bears detailed study, and has a powerful significance.)

19. He would be numbered with the thieves: Isaiah 53:12/Mark 15:27; Luke 22:37.

20. He would be given gall and vinegar: Psalm 69:20, 21/Matt. 237:34; John 19:29.

21. He would suffer alone, with the Father's presence withdrawn: Psalm 22:1, 2/Matt. 27:45, 46.

22. They would cast lots for his garments: Psalm 22:18/John 19:23, 24.

23. He would make intercession for his murderers: Isaiah 53:12/Luke 23:33, 34.

24. His hands and feet would be nailed to the cross: Psalm 22:16/John 20:25.

25. They would break no bone in his body: Psalm 34:20/John 19:32, 33.

26. He would be buried with the rich: Isaiah 53:9/Matt. 27:57-60.

27. His flesh would not see corruption: Psalm 17:9, 10/Acts 2:31.

28. He would ascend into heaven: Psalm 68:18; Dan. 7:13, 14/Eph. 4:8; Acts 2:33-36.

29. He would be the Son of God: Psalm 2:7/Luke 1:31-35.

In the fact of such materials as listed above one must admit that there has to be a high probability that such prophecies and "arranged fulfillments" of them could not have been accomplished by people with only ordinary, natural abilities, when in every case several hundred years separated the prophecy and the fulfillment — even if some dates might be arguable. The prophecies certainly could not have been written as "history, after the event itself had already occurred." The clearest, best and most logical solution to the fact that we truly have such prophecies and fulfillments is to believe that the Holy Spirit of God influenced both the prophet and the fulfilling event, with a definite purpose in mind — to make faith in Jesus as the Christ the Son of God be the most plausible of all the "faith options" that men may have.

CHAPTER 10

Fulfilled Prophecy (Cont'd.)

THE CONVERSION OF PAUL

The Apostle Paul is clearly the most influential Christian in all history. That he lived is not denied. That he wrote several books of the New Testament is not denied, even by the highly critical scholars. Conservatives generally hold that he was the human author of thirteen New Testament books, while Liberals normally allow him from eight to ten. Be that as it may, his book of Romans, for instance, is considered by many to be the most profound and meaningful writing of history. Paul is credited with taking Christianity out into the Gentile world (Roman empire), and thus his influence as God's spokesman is really excelled in western thought only by the person of Jesus himself.

Before Paul was converted to Christianity, however, he was a brilliant young Jew. Educated in Tarsus of Cilicia, probably at a Stoic university, he went to Jerusalem for the finishing of his studies under Gamaliel, the reputed Jewish teacher of the day. In Philippians 3 Paul speaks of his progress and his great opportunities in Judaism, and we could think of no more brilliant future prospects for such a young man. But suddenly he gave up his remarkable progress in the Jewish faith and turned in a complete submission to Christ, where he then "climbed the Christian ladder" to great influence and service.

Question — Why did Paul decide to change from Judaism to Chrisianity and to face the persecution from his former friends that he knew would come to him? He was a brilliant and clear-minded intellectual to begin with, and he was one at the later time also. The Bible gives us the complete story (Acts 9, 22 and 26), and it tells of his personal confrontation with Jesus on the road to Damascus while on his way to persecute Christians.

Liberal theology has a major difficulty in explaining Paul's "conversion" without allowing any contact at all with the supernatural. Paul has been accused of psychological aberrations all the way from migraine headaches to sex-perversion and of any number of illnesses, both mental and physical, in between. His sanity, both before and after the Damascus road experience, however, points to the fact that the conversion was genuine and was a valid intellectual as well as an emotional commitment. No satisfactory explanation has heretofore been offered by those whose presuppositions allow only a naturalistic universe, and in the opinion of this writer, this is a point of difficulty for them where no good explanation is possible.

Biblical Doctrines and Influence

The Judaeo-Christian influence fostered and continued by the Bible has had tremendous salutary effects upon western civilization, giving people a world-view that makes for a better, happier and more abundant life for people in several respects.

The ethical principles proclaimed by Jesus in the Sermon on the Mount are acknowledged even by critics as the world's best ethical program. Our ideal is to become "perfect" (mature) even as God is perfect. To declare that hate and lust are sinful, to expect that the other cheek be turned, to require love of enemies, and that we purify our own lives before we "judge" others, all require a great change in life from all the other patterns of life that men have known of or subscribed to. These Christian ethical principles, when practiced, make a beautiful, happy, altruistic and safe society. Paul's teaching (Phil. 2:3), "Do nothing out of selfish ambition or vain deceit, but in humility consider others better than yourselves," is a similar teaching which puts man's personal ego under a reasoned control, and contributes to a society of such people having an ideal life together.

The Bible's salutary and beneficent effects are well illustrated in the American nation, where it is in fact our sacred book. Despite prolonged efforts of atheists, the Supreme Court has declared us to be a Christian nation, and only recently has refused to take the phrase, "In God We Trust," off of our coins. America was founded by people who desired religious freedom and who wanted to teach the Bible. The Puritans used it as a textbook in their schools, and intellectural life in the early days was enjoyed at the local meetinghouse. The great early schools of the nation were founded to foster Bible study and as pioneers moved out into the west they carried their guns in one hand and the Bible in the other. All this means that the basic world-view and the basic philosophical presuppositions of those who founded our nation and gave it its initial impulse, were derived from the Bible. In spite of the present moral malaise and the disintegration of values that is so obvious today, the basic values subscribed to by the American people are still biblical values, and for this reason, no doubt, we are still the greatest nation in the world, by any way of looking at it. Obviously we need to return to biblical teachings in those ways we have departed or weakened, but the major and basic philosophical views that we still hold today are biblical, such as the value of the individual, the place of human rights, the place of reason in knowing, and the need for a clear-cut authority external to man himself. In no way would we be willing to change our national anthem, so that it would no longer read

> Blest with victory and peace, may the heaven rescued land
>> Praise the Power that hath made and preserved us a
> nation
> Then conquer we must, when our cause it is just,
>> And this be our motto, "In God is our trust."

America's big wars of the present century have all been entered with the purpose of defending individual human rights against the totalitarianism of other systems. To us the government is our servant, not our master. Whereas we appreciate the personality, the equality and the brotherhood of man, we accept Jesus' principle that service is the standard of greatness.

The King James version of the Bible, translated in 1611 A.D. has "made" the English language and preserved it long enough for it to become the major contender as the most popular and most used of the world's languages. Shakespeare quoted the King James version 550 times in his writings and Tennyson 330. Many of the world's greatest orations are sparked with references to it. Lincoln's Gettysburg address points out that, "A house divided against itself cannot stand," while Webster said of Alexander Hamilton, "He smote the rock of national resources and abundant streams of revenue gushed forth." William Jennings Bryan's most famous speech was his "Cross of Gold" speech.

As the world's "best seller" for years, the Bible can energize the individual reader with spiritual power that calls for him to give his life in service to the Lord. It has inspired artists, historians, biographers, travelers, and founders of institutions. The Ten Commandments have become the basis for human law codes.

Our primary philosophical concept of the Bible which men especially appreciate as important is the value of each individual person. Jesus said that one man's soul was more valuable than all the goods of this world, and even those people in our culture who are not spiritually minded recognize the value of each human life. On the day this is being written a five year old girl was rescued unharmed from her kidnapper, and this resuce was played up in the newscasts as a great event, which it is, because all our people recognize the value of any one person's life. Police and the FBI and average citizens were alerted with concern for the child while she was in danger. It was Jesus who gave us this basic concept.

Most Americans appreciate the values inherent in Western civilization in contrast to some of those in the Far East or the Third World. Democracy thrives, individual opportunity is possible, and concern for the "have-nots" are basic to our outlook, and we would have it no other way. In so many cultures, people feel that it is "every man for himself, and the devil take the hindmost."

CHAPTER 11

THE UNITY OF THE BIBLE

Why did God create man, and why the universe? 1 Corinthians 10:31 says, "whatsoever you do, do all to the glory of God," and Ephesians 3:20, speaking of the Father, says, "unto him be the glory in the church and in Christ Jesus unto all generations forever and ever.

Since Jehovah is a person, it is quite understandable that he would want communion, fellowship and love from other persons. Of course Jesus and the Holy Spirit are also persons, but they too are God and someway are one with him, so that the desirability for communion with other persons still remains. Man was created and, although he *is* a person, he is less than God and has severe limitations. One thing man should do is to respect reality — namely that God is a higher being and this is to be acknowledged in worship and in giving due homage to the Father-Creator, which includes "glorifying" him. In brief, we might say that God created man because he wanted someone to love, and to love him.

True personhood can exist only among free-moral agents, that is, persons who are free to choose without coercion. Yet motivations to do both good or evil are valid and fair, so Satan was given permission to tempt man. We well understand that sooner or later man will sin, and since the Father, by his very nature cannot tolerate sin in his presence, all sin must be forgiven if one is to have God's final approval.

The Father's purpose through the ages then, and even from the beginning, was to provide a way for sinful man to have redemption, since he knew that man would sin. Passages that indicate that he foreknew and planned for human redemption from the beginning include:

1 Peter 1:19, 20 — ". . . but with precious blood, as of a lamb without blemish and without spot, even the blood of Christ, who was foreknown indeed before the foundation of the world, but was manifested at the end of the times . . ."

Revelation 13:8 (footnote) — "slain from the foundation of the world."

Ephesians 3:9-11 — ". . . the dispensation of the mystery which for ages hath been hid in God . . . might be made known through the church the manifold wisdom of God, according to the eternal purpose which he purposed in Christ Jesus our Lord . . ."

In view of the overall plan and purpose of God as indicated above, we are not surprised at the covenant God made with Abraham, as he moved to implement his overall plan for the redemption of man from sin — "in thee shall all the families of the earth be blessed" (Gen. 12:3; see also Gal. 3:16). This Abrahamic covenant interlocks with several other specific and individual covenants made for special purposes, and all of them together work out and unfold into God's grand plan of redemption that culminated in the Christian system.

These several covenants deserve some special mention because of their importance in the overall plan:

First, there was the Patriarchal period, when "father rule" was the normal pattern for God's people. This period began with Adam, and in it the father of a family was dominant over all his descendants — religiously, politically, and in other ways. At the death of the patriarch the birthright (i.e., leadership in the tribe and a double portion of the estate) passed to the eldest male child. It was the duty of the patriarch to teach God's will to his descendants, and divine "revelations" came to him from time to time "in many and various ways" (Heb. 1:1). Human reason and judgment leading to "a law unto themselves" were used in formulating practical rules for living (Rom. 2:12-16), where specific and written divine revelation was not present.

A second prominent covenant in God's plan is the Abrahamic, noted above and which is delineated to some degree in Genesis 12:1-3. It has numerous promises — four of which are fulfilled in the physical Jewish nation who were God's chosen people during this period. This passage gives them the promise of a great name, and that they should be a great nation. They were promised the land of Palestine as their homeland for the duration of this covenant and from Genesis 17 we find the practice of circumcision given as an identifying obligation to people of the covenant. All four these factors were "earthly" (pertaining to physical life) and were thus empirically realized. They were all brought to complete fulfillment in the Jewish nation before the time of Christ, and therefore have no part in the New Covenant of Christ. The *spiritual* promise of the Abrahamic covenant, however, is the basic thread (salvation for all families of the earth) that continues on, and, though dormant during the Mosaic period, comes into its full realization in the Christian covenant. This is fulfilled in "the seed" or posterity of Abraham, which Galatians 3:16 says is Christ himself. So the promise of victory for "the woman's seed" (Gen. 3:15) is renewed to Abraham (Gen. 12:3) and is finally realized when Christ's atoning death on the cross brought the New Covenant into fulfillment with its beginning on Pentecost day (Acts 2).

The Mosaic covenant is the one given at Mount Sinai and consisted in laws of which the Ten Commandments are the nucleus. It has laws governing worship and ceremonial obligations of the individual in his relation to God, but it also had numerous rules and regulations governing the civil obligations of the Jewish citizens to each other and to outsiders. The law of Moses could not take away sin because that is not possible by law alone, and is not the purpose of law anyway (see Rom. 3:20, 28; Gal. 2:16, 20; 3:11, 21). Since a "law" covenant cannot as a mere "list of rules" accomplish what is really needed for humanity, the absolute forgiveness of sins; and since it had only animal sacrifices (see Heb. 10:4), the purpose of the Mosaic covenant was only temporary to begin with (see Gal. 3:24 for a statement of this). It served to take care of the needs of the Jewish people during the time the covenant was valid, but it was originally understood and planned that it should ultimately be done away with and superseded. Passages which in their contexts declare this positively are:

> Ephesians 2:14 — "For he is our peace, who made both one, and brake down the middle wall of partition, having abolished in his flesh the enmity, even the law of commandments contained in ordinances . . ."

> Colossians 2:14 — ". . . having blotted out the bond written in ordinances that was against us, which was contrary to us: and he hath taken it out of the way, nailing it to the cross . . ."

Jeremiah 31:31-34 and Hebrews 8:6-12 — "Behold the days come, saith Jehovah, that I will make a new covenant with the house of Israel, and with the house of Judah: not according to the covenant that I made with their fathers in the day that I took them by the hand to bring them out of the land of Egypt . . . *et cetera.*"

"The middle wall of partition" (the law) had separated the Gentiles and Jews during the time of operation of the Mosaic covenant, but after Christianity began Jews and Gentiles are admitted into the church upon the same terms (see Acts 11:19 and 19:34, 35). In Christianity the spiritual promise given to Abraham became a reality and thus "all families" of the earth are now eligible for its spiritual benefits which are made available through the cross of Christ and because of his atoning death as our sin-offering.

By contrast with the law of Moses, which in essence could be no more than mere "law," the Christian system is a "grace" religion. The principle of justification under the Mosaic code was human merit, which meant perfect obedience (see Phil. 3:8, 9; Gal. 3:10; James 2:10). But perfect obedience is found only in Jesus' life (Rom. 3:23), so the rest of us need mercy and forgiveness — above all. The law had no Saviour but Christianity does, and God's grace and mercy are now available to us on the basis of faith, in spite of the fact that we have not earned them nor do we deserve them. Human merit does not enter the picture.

The spiritual covenant made with Abraham is a more significant covenant than was Moses' law, even though practically all of the Old Testament is taken up with the history of the Jews under that program. Christianity is God's spiritual fulfillment of salvation for "all families," which is available nowhere else, and since in it the Abrahamic promise becomes realized, the technical place of the Mosaic covenant is that "it was added (to the Abrahamic covenant) because of transgressions, till the seed should come to whom the promise hath been made" (Gal. 3:19). Thus the Mosaic law, originally, and in the development of God's major plan of redemption for humanity, was not a necessity in an integral sense, but was added to take care of the needs of the Jews as a people and in their relations with others, and do only *until the coming of Christ* and the inauguration of the New Covenant of Jesus Christ. It was temporary in its planning, and its demise was built-in from the start. The good Bible scholar of today, therefore, should know the place of the Mosaic covenant in relation to the entire plan of redemption, and should thus be "able to rightly divide the word" in his studies (2 Tim. 2:15).

Relation of the Testaments

We wish to discuss even further the relation of the Old and New Testaments in view of the fact that in the public mind there is a dearth of clear, incisive knowledge about the relationship. Not only the general public, but many religious teachers in the denominations and also trained philosophers who make comments and have conclusions about the significance and the place of the Bible, all find themselves woefully ignorant of God's plan of redemption as it is developed in the Old and New Testaments, and many are totally unable to intelligently "rightly divide the word of truth" (2 Tim. 2:15). It is somewhat sad, for instance, to read from "professional" religious teachers who think that the Old Covenant is as binding today as it ever was who feel that the church is as much of an Old Testament institution as it is a Christian one.

The Old Testament is the Jewish book of scriptures that relates the origins of man and the universe and the pre-Abrahamic history. After Abraham, and in order to bring to realization the promise of redemption for "all families," God chose that Abraham should be the father of a physical nation, to be fostered and to develop as his chosen people in distinction from other tribes and peoples. To this Jewish nation, after they were called out from Egyptian bondage, was given the Law of Moses, of which the Ten Commandments was the nucleus, but numerous other precepts and requirements were given for them to follow.

The Law had an elaborate sacrificial and worship system which embraced all their obligations and relations to God. It also had a detailed set of "civil statutes," which comprehensively covered the relations of the Jews to each other and to their neighboring tribes. Then again there were obligations of behavior where only self was involved, but a violation of any of the legal obligations was a sin against God. All commandments comprehended under the law were "carnal ordinances, imposed until a time of reformation" (Heb. 9:10), and this type of law was basically ineffective for man's real spiritual needs, as the two previous verses (8 and 9) say — "the Holy Spirit this signifying, that the way into the holy place hath not yet been made manifest, while the first tabernacle is yet standing; which is a figure for the time present; according to which are offered both gifts and sacrifices that cannot, as touching the conscience, make the worshipper perfect . . ."

More specifically, animal sacrifices, which is all the Law of Moses had, are not adequate atonement for sin. Hebrews 10:4 notes, "For it is impossible that the blood of bulls and goats should take away sins." Sin against God is so bad that its punishment means separation from God throughout eternity, further, it is so heinous that it requires the death of God's Son to overcome its impact. This still is to allow for God's love all the while. Sin is just that bad by nature. It is difficult for the ordinary human to comprehend this, since we ourselves are sinners. (One would hardly expect a jury of murderers to be able to fairly fix the punishment for murder.)

The logical conclusion to the teaching about the Law of Moses in the Old Testament is that it was given in the first place as a temporary measure, and it of itself could not provide for man's real need but could only give types and foreshadowings of the real, true, efficacious religious system that Christ was to bring when he came into the world "in the fulness of time" (Gal. 4:4). It was preplanned that the law would end as the binding covenant of God with his people. To fail to understand this will issue in being unable to "rightly divide the word" and therefore to fail to get the basic message of the Bible — that Christ is our "sin-offering," and that only in him is there any hope of forgiveness for sinful man (see Rom. 3:25; Gal. 2:20).

The New Covenant

What the law was unable to do, God did through Christ:

Rom. 8:2-4 — For the law of the Spirit of life in Christ Jesus made me free from the law of sin and death. For what the law could not do, in that it was weak through the flesh, God, sending his own Son in the likeness of sinful flesh and for sin, condemned sin in the flesh; that the ordinance of the law might be fulfilled in us, who walk not after the flesh, but after the Spirit.

Prophecy in abundance was given in the Old Testament as to the nature and function of the New Covenant, and it finds detailed fulfillment in the New. The passages mentioned earlier from Jeremiah 31:31f and Hebrews 8:6ff are as good illustrations as anyone should need of this point that God originally planned the New Covenant as the fulfillment and replacement of the Old, and that it should provide that which was ultimate for meeting the human need of forgiveness of sins.

The book of Hebrews presents in more detail then any other New Testament book the fact that the Law of Moses as a religious system could not bring redemption to sinful man, and that the Christian system — one of grace and complete forgiveness — could do this. Thus Christ is presented as the ultimate atonement, and he needed to be offered only "once for all" (see Heb. 7:27; 9:7, 12, 15, 25, 26; 10:3, 11, 12), as versus the animal sacrifices of the Old Covenant which had to be offered repeatedly, once each year (Heb. 9:25; 10:11). Those sacrifices were not effective and, in fact, were nothing more than types of the later atonement of Christ.

Whereas under the law, any reward was based upon human deserving, (Phil. 3:8, 9), the Christian system offers a salvation based upon Christ's merit and is therefore a gift to man (see Eph. 2:8; Rom. 6:23). In a real sense, therefore, the nature of the New Covenant is that it is "non-legal." By this we mean that it is not based upon mere "rule keeping" of the individual, but is based upon his faith in, trust of, and dependence upon the blood atonement of Jesus Christ. When we face the judgment bar in the last great day we shall be able to "be clothed in the robes of Christ's righteousness," not in the rags of our own merit. Since salvation is a gift, the Christian system is a grace program and one that allows God to exercise mercy rather than the justice that we deserve.

We do not know why "blood" is such a powerful atonement for sin, but God has so declared it. It may be because it embraces life itself, so that when Christ died on the cross he gave himself. He, as God, died the shameful and ignominious death of the cross for us, and in which he expressed an ultimate quality of love for us, even though we were yet sinners. Probably nothing else could arouse a love and confidence in return, to make hardened sinners yield themselves in humble submission to his will. When this occurs the new Christian reaches his greatest possible spiritual zenith and he becomes unselfish and filled with love for God and for his fellowman.

The Place of the Old Testament Today

Since the Old Covenant was "nailed to the cross" and has now been taken away, it behooves us in "rightly dividing the word" to recognize this fact and to understand that only the New Covenant is God's revealed will for the Christian age. We observe today only New Covenant obligations; however, we must realize that a great many precepts of the Old Covenant age are also found incorporated into the New, so that we today must obey many commands that are found in the Old Testament, but we do so because they are also a part of the New. These include such matters as faith in God, worship and obedience to his will, and numerous other obligations. Things that we should not do today which were a part of the Old Covenant requirements but which are not found in the New are: animal sacrifices; tithing; keeping the Sabbath day (Saturday) holy; instrumental music in public worship; the keeping of certain Jewish vows, Jewish holidays, and similar matters.

It so happens that nine of the original Ten Commandments are in principle found in the New Covenant, but we do not keep the Ten Commandments "as such," because they are not, as a corporate list, part of the New Testament teaching.

Romans 15:4 states that "whatsoever things were written aforetime were written for our learning, that through patience and through comfort of the scriptures we might have hope." The Old Testament therefore is valuable to the Christian today as a history of God's dealings with his people of a former age, and it shows the unfolding of the great plan of salvation which culminates in Christ. It was inspired in its production and is God's word, as it served as God's law for the Jewish age. Now that that age is ended and all of its "physical" promises found in the Abrahamic covenant have been fulfilled — the spiritual promise of salvation for "all families" being the only thing yet to be fulfilled in Christ (Gal. 3:16) — we turn to the New Testament for instruction and guidance and expressions of the Lord's will for us in the Christian age, but we respect and read the Old Testament for information, instruction and inspiration as it throws light on New Testament principles.

Unity

That there is a unity in the Bible and between the two major Testaments is openly demonstrated in the thousand or more quotations and allusions found in the New, taken from the Old. Further, the many prophecies that we have been discussing could not exist without there being a definite, clear plan of interrelationship and unity. Yet again, the clear view of the unfolding of God's master plan of redemption through the various covenants from the creation all the way through to the presentation of the Christian system, is in fact documentation of the unity of the whole.

Jesus Christ as "the seed of the woman" (Gen 3:15); as Abraham's "seed" through whom the spiritual promise to him was to be realized (Gal. 3:16); as the lawgiver for whom Moses was the type (Acts 3:22); as the effective blood atonement (Heb. 9:11-14), demonstrates to any and all who seek a reasonable faith, that the two Testaments are unified in all their relationships, even though they present two distinct religions with different principles.

BIBLICAL INTERPRETATION

CHAPTER 12
THE CRITICAL APPROACH

Several factors in history have contributed to the arrival of many of the modern views toward the Bible and its interpretation. During the Dark Ages people had little education and so superstitions and numerous forms of imaginings held sway as to their basic outlook on life. When education began again and universities were founded, the Renaissance ("rebirth") period enlarged their intellectual horizons and opportunities. Many old manuscripts were found and they began to realize something of the great learning of former days and the "yen to learn" took on an enthusiasm. Out of this spirit authorities such as the papacy and the general councils of the Catholic church began to be questioned, and so we have the beginning of the Protestant Reformation. Humanists and philosophers also delved into new ideas in their realms, and soon we find "scientific" thought beginning in a serious way. Francis Bacon formulated a systematic statement about inductive reasoning, and before long it evolved into a full-fledged "scientific method" of approaching problems, which method, as it further developed, has brought to man the many gains that science has made available to us in the past three hundred years. With these gains in science, and the great emphasis on "cause-effect relations" that science fosters, has now come a much stronger appreciation of naturalism as the one true basic philosophic outlook. The supernaturalism found in miracles and inspiration, accepted by Christianity through the ages, now began to be suspect for many; and science, coupled with naturalism, began to replace it as a "religion" for numerous people.

Theology did not escape this new appreciation for the gains from the scientific method, so Bible study began to be approached "scientifically;" but what is new and questionable, is that it was done with the presupposition of an *antisupernaturalism.* Such an approach formed the theological stance of Liberalism, for those who followed it, and its method when fully developed became known as the "historical method," or, "the historical-critical method." The word "criticism" in Bible study does not today necessarily imply *antagonism* to traditional conclusions. It simply means a thorough investigation of all possible facts, with an objective, "scientific" attitude. There can be nothing wrong with this, as such. Most people who willingly wear the label "critic," however, also assume a basic naturalistic philosophy, as versus being willing to consider the possibility of supernaturalism. This is the basis of the change to "modernism."

The historical-critical method of itself seeks out facts, from areas such as exegesis, archaeology, history, and other similar areas which might throw any light upon the biblical topic under study. These, of course, are legitimate questions, because they deal with factural reality and with matters as they actually are. It is not scientific, however, to dismiss miracles, inspiration of scripture, or other expressions of supernatural power as not possible, purely under the assumption that "natural law" can explain all reality and historical events, without any help from outside sources. It is nothing but an assumption to think that our universe is completely self enclosed, up to the point where science's knowledge ends, and that God, if he exists, never enters our sphere of activity or influences it in any way. It is clearly and logically possible for God to act within the sphere of human action. There is no way to be certain that natural law, or physical cause-effect forces, are all that there is. If there could be a God who could create a universe like ours, then for him to intervene beneficently in the workings of nature without disrupting them would be no problem at all.

In the preface to the second edition of his commentary on Romans, Karl Barth about 1922 challenged the historical critical method of Bible study as the Liberals were then employing it, and he furnished a clue which finally shows the method to be impossible as the exlusive and final arbiter of the meaning of the Bible. He pointed out that there are many great and important questions that historical criticism cannot touch, such matters as "Messianic consciousness;" Paul's purpose in writing; the why, and the meaning of it all. Grammatical niceties and empirical data do not explain these, yet they also deal with reality and with problems which must be answered. This, then, was part of the beginning of Liberalism's demise as a major theological option, and it has been dying since that time. There are few strict Liberals in theology today.

Accompanying the critical historical method as the method "par-excellence" of Liberalism was the "Hegelian philosophy of history" which holds that history itself is no more than the result of the clash of evolving ideas, with continuing progress and gain in knowledge, such as education and science can provide. There is for Hegel an Absolute, the ultimate truth, from which derives a cosmic force or power that causes the process or the ongoingness of history.[28] This concept of "evolving ideas," caused by a natural process and bringing continuing progress, thus furnished a compatible companion to the naturalistic, "scientific approach to Bible study" of the historical method, and these together came to be counted as companion points of faith for Liberal thinkers. Also the claim of evolution of biological species, of the Darwinian type, fitted nicely into this pattern of reality. Darwin issued his *Origin of the Species* in 1859, and heavy inroads were then made upon traditional conservative beliefs held generally by Christianity concerning creation and other supernatural activity. This was possible only because Hegel had been widely accepted.

A major conclusion of the critics then was that the Bible could not withstand the tests of valid criticism, and therefore could not be the authoritative word of God. They decided that it had too many discrepancies and errors, and the recognition of differing vocabularies in the Greek text of the several books was in their view the final straw that proved that the Bible is only a human book.

Since Higher Criticism is committed to the basic philosophy of naturalism, and all their conclusions are colored by that basic outlook, we are not surprised that all problems of introduction, exegesis and similar matters for them are also determined within that particular framework. For instance, the relationships among the Synoptic gospels have to be studied and determined from a naturalistic presupposition. No impact or

---

[28]See Vol. I, pp. 20-22 for a fuller discussion of Hegel.

influence of the Holy Spirit whatever can be considered. If necessary, history must be distorted; difficult passages are declared to be later interpolations and thus must be ignored; or some other conclusion compatible with naturalism must be reached.

CHAPTER 13

LITERARY CRITICISM

Literary Criticism is the name generally used to describe the historical study of complete documents (as the gospels) and this designation is used because they are complete pieces of literature. For example we study Mark's gospel in relation to Matthew's as whole documents. It has been concluded for years by higher critics that Mark wrote first, and Matthew and Luke copied from him. The facts faced are that the three gospels have strong likenesses in certain passages, even word for word, while they vary greatly at other points. For those passages where Matthew and Luke (but not Mark) have very close agreement in wording, it has been *assumed* that there was another document, now lost, from which Matthew and Luke both copied. This "lost" document, for which there is no manuscript evidence, is called "Q" for the German word, *Quelle,* which means "source." Since no one had ever heard of Q until the need for it (under this naturalistic pressure) developed in literary criticism, it must remain suspect as a valid document. In fact, there has arisen in recent years a serious question even upon the part of some critical scholars as to whether Mark was really written first. If Markan priority should fall, it will reopen the whole matter of literary criticism of the Synoptics for the higher critics. There are numerous other problems of this type where criticism is under heavy pressure to reach certain conclusions, in spite of the demand that the known facts have to be strained. Many date the writing of Mark firmly at 70 A.D., because in Mark 13 specific details are given by Jesus about the fall of Jerusalem, which occurred in August of that year. As the critic sees it, Jesus could not have made this statement, because it would have been a supernatural prophecy, and critics therefore want the passage written *after* the event, as history, which is compatible to naturalism. But for it to have been written later would make it difficult for Matthew and Luke to have copied from it, within a reasonable date for them. Thus the strained conclusion as to a precise date.

Form Criticism is the name of the next critical approach to the study of the gospels, which has as its goal to find out exactly what Jesus said and did, since it is presupposed that the gospels themselves do not furnish factual history. A "form" is a small segment or pericope in a gospel which more or less stands alone and is connected to the rest of the material by transitional words. Critical study of these forms (such as an "I" saying, a healing narrative, a miracle story, etc.) is to look into their history and development, probable origin, etc. All this can be a valid study, insofar as the scholar does not arbitrarily reach conclusions that are not supported by facts. The truth of the matter is that even though some new valid information is learned, the great majority of form critical study is done under strong naturalistic influences and under great stress to find naturalistic explanations for the facts learned. This is neither scientific nor scholarly, and certainly is not a proper basis for religious faith.

CHAPTER 14

CHRISTOLOGY

Ever since the experience at Caesarea Philippi when Jesus asked his disciples, "Who do men say that I the Son of man am?" this has proved to be *the* important question for Christian faith. The answer that Peter gave — "Thou art the Christ, the Son of the living God," is not accepted by naturalistically inclined scholars, who strive diligently to avoid answers which imply the supernatural.

Since our present calendar has a four year mistake in it, we say that Jesus was crucified in 29 A.D., and from that date to 70 A.D. when Mark's gospel was written, according to these scholars, there *evolved* in the early Christian community the concept that Jesus was divine. In 29 no one thought him to be divine, but in 70 he was definitely preached as a divine-human. During these 41 years this complete change-over took place, all conceived and carried out by his followers. Liberals completely reject Jesus as a divine being since they are scientifically and naturalistically minded and therefore hold that for the Christ to be thought of as divine is pure fiction and unworthy of consideration. Neo-Orthodox or existentialist scholars, on the other hand, think of the earthly Jesus as unimportant, and yet the "God-man concept" which was held "as early as 70 A.D." is the greatest religious idea that has every been known. Liberals are thus interested in "the historical Jesus" who was but a mere man yet a truly religious "genius;" while the Neo-Orthodox theologians have no interest in the Jesus of history but feel that the "Christ of faith" (the *faith* of the early Christian community of 70 A.D. onward) should be the central focus of Christianity.

Both of these major theologies of the twentieth century therefore reject Jesus as God's divine Son, as do numerous others. But their naturalistic conclusions do not adequately allow for certain facts. It takes more than human religious genius to explain Jesus' power and influence. The time factor is not well accounted for by naturalistic theories. It took some time after the resurrection in their view for the followers to decide to stay together and to begin to preach the importance of Jesus. We may assume that it would be about 35 A.D. before they worked out such a plan. Then Paul's letters, beginning in 50 A.D. with the writing of 1 Thessalonians, recognize Jesus as fully divine, and they were written to congregations of Christians, fully established, that already knew the gospel story about him and had accepted his divinity. In other words, the divinity of Jesus was not first held in the year 70 A.D., but long before, since Paul would had to have written a gospel himself if his readers had not already known about Jesus as the Son of God. So we have only from 35-50 A.D. for this marvelous concept to have evolved, if it in fact did, and 15 years is not enough time for such as this to occur. There were eyewitnesses, both friendly and unfriendly, who knew much about Jesus' teachings and works, and who lived through this entire period. So it is preposterous to conclude that no one conceived of Jesus as divine during his lifetime, but that many accepted such as a fact by 70 A.D., and all this without any miracles, inspiration or supernatural influence whatever!

CHAPTER 15

ESCHATOLOGY AND ETHICS

In studying the history of the "search for the real Jesus" on the part of critical scholars we find that great attention came to the problem in the book by Albert Schweitzer, *The Quest of the Historical Jesus,* published in 1906. Schweitzer, himself a liberal, challenged the previous conclusions of liberalism that Jesus was "a good guy" with the world's best ethical code, albeit only human. Schweitzer personally decided that Jesus was a sort of religious fanatic, who actually thought that he would indeed "come back on the clouds and set up his kingdom." The superior ethic of the Sermon on the Mount was for Schweitzer only an "Interimsethik," but he was scholarly enough to challenge Liberalism effectively to reexamine its own conclusions, and he thus threw the whole problem open to new study by them. This study has continued since that day, but with little results so far to show for it.

C. H. Dodd of Great Britain about 1940 came up with a new idea, that of "realized eschatology," which argues that Jesus believed that the kingdom was not futuristic, but was already realized — that is to say, God's people on earth were already a reality in the present time, not just at some time in the future. Dodd's argument has enough scriptural support that it gained considerable following, and critical scholarship is still divided at the present time as to what Jesus really did teach on the subject. The present writer holds that the scripture teaches that the kingdom, in Jesus' view, is both present today (in the church, the body of Christ) and in the future (following the judgment day). The scriptural teachings on the point bear this out.

Admittedly the ethical or moral principles contained in the Sermon on the Mount is the loftiest ethical code known to men. Critics acknowledge this, and it is a problem to them to explain it without acknowledging a supernatural influence. Of course many of the "bricks" of Jesus' teaching are found in earlier traditions, but even so, the "mortar" which holds them together are admittedly his, and thus he produced fresh, new principles. Nothing is known to equal his ethical standards, and without doubt he is the Master Teacher of all time.

CHAPTER 16

KERYGMA AND MYTH

Kerygma and Myth are fairly recent terms that have been injected into the discussions about what Jesus really said and did. Both words have two common meanings among the scholars. Kerygma is a Greek term meaning the "first principles declaration" or "heralding" of the basic message about Jesus and his work. Myth is normally understood to be an untrue account of a happening, for whatever purpose. Rudolf Bultmann was an existentialist scholar and theologian who attracted considerable attention by arguing that the New Testament was written in mythological terms of the first century, in their thought forms which are not applicable today. In other words, the New Testament people thought of heaven as "up," hell as "down," of the "four corners of the world" and any number of other similar expressions which our modern knowledge has proved to be wrong and literally untenable. These first century forms are "myth" (in Bultmann's definition), and cannot have meaning for twentieth century people until they are "demythed" or translated into a proper twentieth century terminology. This is a good illustration of where existentialism shows its high subjectivity. Jesus' "resurrection" does not mean the literal resuscitation of a corpse, but rather means in Bultmann's view that "I can come alive to God in Christ." And this would be done in an existential sense. To explain all this understandably cannot be done, because this philosophy opposes reason to begin with. In the view of the present writer, this is no interpretation of the Bible at all.

Since all critical scholars have concluded that the gospels are not true history and cannot be depended upon, the question remains, where shall we go to learn about the true Jesus and what he said and did? The question is still unsolved for them. But for the Bible believer the gospels are true historical accounts and we have no problems with miracles or other supernatural events as they are presented understandably in the pages of the New Testament. Jesus is God's Son and the New Testament is the inspired record of his revelation to us of his deeds, sayings, and specific expressions of his commands for us. The Christian religion takes on a full meaning for each person as he is born into God's family, commits himself to live for the Lord and starts out on the new spiritual life in the body of Christ.

C. H. Dodd, while accepting that the gospels are not dependable history, decided that the place to find the truth about Jesus was in the basic preaching, the *kerygma*, (here rightly defined) of the apostles as found in the sermons recorded in the book of Acts. This view has not been overwhelmingly accepted, so the puzzle still remains for critics as to what we should decide about Jesus, what we can truly know about him.

CHAPTER 17

NORMATIVE INTERPRETATION

To follow critical scholarship very far, with all its naturalistic presuppositions, would cause one to find himself "out in left field." A more refreshing view is to look at the New Testament as a book, like any other book, to be read, reasoned upon, and understood — then believed and obeyed. To think that God could not have given us his revelation in terms that the normal man can comprehend, just as he can understand a history book or an arithmetic book, is to imagine things about God that are not simple and reasonable. God made us, knows our nature, can communicate with us on our level of ability, and there is no reason at all to feel that he did not do just that.

Most men use the inductive method of reasoning, even though we do not know this descriptive term. This is how we normally think, reasoning from the specific to the general. We find an hypothesis that explains all the specific facts related to our problem and thus conclude that this is the answer.

Again, the normal use of language, giving full recognition to grammatical principles as they would apply in normal human communication, and the use of historical facts as they are determined, give us what is called the grammatical-historical method of interpretation. There are other features that come into consideration in biblical interpretation, just as they do in all human communication, but these are to be "played by ear" as they appear and do not affect the overall method that is proper. What we are saying is that normal biblical interpretation is not at all as complicated as most scholars want to make it. It needs to be done carefully and with due deference to linguistic and texual demands, as good scholarly investigation indicates. It should take into account all matters such as figurative language (which is freely used in everyday communication), and peculiarities of the Greek language such as idioms. But when it is all said and done the normal person should be able to get the basic message from the text by himself. Commentaries and special studies can help to elucidate the more difficult matters but what a person needs to do to become a Christian and to live a life well-pleasing unto the Father should be considered as knowable by the ordinary person without any unusual or special help.

The tendency to reject the supernatural influences that are so obvious in the scriptures has not always been with us. As we noted, earlier, the rise of science in the past three hundred years, and with this the stronger appreciation of the operation of natural law, have together caused many to feel that the powerful laws of nature are all the powers there are, and that they are adequate to explain all that man needs to be concerned with. There is no reason, however, to deny the supernatural influences that the Bible presents. That the Creator God could intervene in the operation of nature's laws should be no problem at all, since he is also the author of nature itself. There is no supernatural influence mentioned in scripture that is pre-posterous or utterly impossible to accept. Hebrews 2:4 declares that God "bears witness" of confirmation of the teaching of the apostles "by signs, wonders, manifold powers, and gifts of the Holy Spirit," and Mark 16:20 observes that the Lord "confirmed the word by the signs that followed." So there was a definite purpose for such supernatural usages. There were many persons in those days who claimed to have supernatural abilities, and when God's true spokesman could really invoke healings, speak in foreign languages, and other signs that were unquestionably not natural or ordinary happenings, this was a confirmation of the spokesman's message. This was the purpose of miracles in the early days of the church. The ability to "work" such powers was limited to the apostles (Acts 1:8), and those upon whom the apostles conferred the gift by the laying on of their hands (Acts 8:15-18). When the last apostle died and the last person died upon whom gifts had been conferred, that was the end of miracles in the Christian age, because their purpose had been fully served. By that time the Bible had been written and it today serves as its own confirmation, through the fulfillment of prophecy and similar indications that it is more than just a human book.

To the average man of today it should be obvious that there is more to reality than is observable through the senses. There must have been a mind that organized this highly complex universe, which happens to be so beautifully habitable by man and so suitable for his needs. His moral conscience is not subject to scientific investigation, yet it is a powerful reality with which he must reckon. The scientists can answer questions as to what and when and how, and even as to who and where, but they are completely baffled by the question of "Why?" Yet there must be a why! To hold that the universe is here by mere chance, with all its organization so logical that the human mind can gradually come to understand it as scientists have come to discover new truths, requires more gullibility than to believe that the Creator God who is a person, made the universe for a purpose, and that man as his crowning creature has a special place and function in his plan.

CHAPTER 18

INTERPRET AS ORDINARY LANGUAGE
OR LITERATURE

Many critical scholars insist that the Bible should be interpreted as any other book, but when they say this they probably mean that the reader should reject all supernaturalism as a beginning presupposition. To be sure we look at the average *novel* of our day as written under completely natural circumstances. And we would expect no new absolute moral pronouncements in such a volume. When an ordinary human writing uses the word *God* we might understand that an "impersonal cosmic force" is what he means. *God* has many definitions in human philosophy and among the several human religions. But when "God" is used in the Bible it takes on a specific meaning — Jehovah, the God of Abraham, Isaac and Jacob, and later, "the Father of our Lord Jesus Christ."

To say, therefore, that "we should study the Bible as any other book," and mean by that that when the word *God* occurs we should understand only some sort of an impersonal cosmic force, or the meaning of the term in Zen Buddhism or in Marxist philosophy, would not be fair or legitimate in any way of looking at it.

The true way of "studying the Bible as any other book: is to let the laws of language take their normal course. Human beings, communicate their meanings to each other through language, and all languages have parts of speech — nouns, verbs, prepositions, etc. Contexts play a large part in human communication and certainly this is true in biblical interpretation. Immediate context, larger context, and even the entire Bible with its covenants and overall plan of redemption must all be taken into account in anything like a correct interpretation. The word must be rightly divided.

The uses of the same words that one is trying to interpret, by the same author in other New Testament passages, and in the entire culture of the same period can guide one helpfully. The historical circumstances of the writing, the customs and manners of the time in question and the purpose of the author will all furnish valuable clues to the intended meaning. Actually, men have little trouble in ordinary human communication in getting the intended meanings, and, unless there is a special reason in a given instance, we can all get the meaning that was intended in the writing of the Bible without an special difficulty.

Probably the worst trouble about knowing the Bible is the lack of real serious study of it. Often when it is studied, meanings are read into it which are not really there. The open-minded stance with an humble, earnest desire to know allows the best assurance of clearly getting God's truth.

There are different methods of approaching scripture to get at its meaning. One is literal interpretation, to take it word for word for what it says. Many religions overdo the literal approach when there are good reasons for considering something as figurative. Critics usually ridicule this practice, and condemn all conservative interpreters for being guilty of this even when they are quite reasonable about literal language. Obviously some language is intended to be literal and should be taken that way. Actually, interpretation is an art, and much study needs to go into its finer nuances, even though ordinary meanings are easily known.

Again, figurative language, with the several figures of speech and thought that are possible, is a standard practice in all human communication, and the Bible uses figurative language just like any other medium of communication. That Jesus is a lamb, is easily understood as a figure of speech; and, "wolves shall arise from among your own selves" is another that requires no difficulty in interpretation. Common sense is a requisite in understanding any human communication, and is also needed in knowing the word of God, for God gave his message in an ordinary human language form.

Examples

Logic indicates that special revelation in scripture may come through direct commands or teachings, through necessary inferences, and through examples of conduct or attitude that appear in the context to be approved. That exemplary conduct does teach either approved or disapproved conduct is obvious in all walks of life. A parent teaches his child in this manner, so does the professional teacher, the boss, the superior in the military or in any other human relationship. Oftentimes the parent, by bad behaviour himself, teaches his child the same bad behaviour, and when he tries to correct it, he says, "Don't do as I do; do as I say." We have all heard this and know that it is true. Some biblical passages that illustrate this point are:

Phil. 3:17 — Brethren, join in imitating me, and mark those who so live as you have an example in us.

Phil. 4:9 — What you have learned and received and heard and seen in me, do; and the God of peace will be with you.

1 Cor. 8:10 — For if anyone sees you, a man of knowledge, at table in an idol's temple, might he not be encouraged, if his conscience is weak, to eat food offered to idols?

1 Cor. 10:6 — Now these things are warnings for us, not to desire evil as they did.

1 Cor. 11:1 — Be imitators of me, as I am of Christ.

2 Thess. 3:9 — It was not because we did not have that right, but to give you in our conduct an example to imitate.

1 Peter 3:1, 2 — Likewise you wives, be submissive to your husbands, so that some, though they dod not obey the word, may be won without the word by the behaviour of their wives, when they see your reverent and chaste behaviour.

Matt. 5:16 — Let your light so shine before men, that they may see your good works and give glory to your Father who is in heave.

What an example teaches is what it is an example of. If the exemplary conduct is of something that was optional to the Christian then, it teaches that the same conduct is optional today. But if it is an example of something the biblical character of that day as a Christian was required to do, then we today are required to do the same thing. The principle is simple — what people of New Testament times had to do to be well pleasing unto God, we have to do today to gain the same approval.

It is true that not many major interpretations of consequence are dependent upon the teaching of examples of conduct found in scripture, but there are some.

THE NEW TESTAMENT
MESSAGE

CHAPTER 19

CHRISTIANITY A UNIQUE RELIGION

When all is said and done about the place and purpose of the Bible, and about the proper methodology for determining its exact meanings it still resolves down to the fact that what is important about it at all is its message. Romans 10:17 says, "Faith comes by hearing and hearing by the message of Christ." It is the *content* of the message, *what* a person comes to believe, that makes all the difference in the world between religions.

Christianity is unique among the religions of the world in that it is monotheistic, universal and ethical, all at the same time. It as a religion gives full glory and credit to God and recognizes man's subordinate relation to him as his creature, and thus boldly faces reality, yet it allows a high value for man. He is made in God's image, and thus is the highest of the creatures, and as a person man has some of the same capacities that God has, such as the capacity to love, to reason at a comparatively high level, and to have both freedom and responsibility for his moral decisions. As a person man can have interpersonal relationships with the Godhead. Christians are adopted into God's spiritual family and we can share in loving family intimacies with our Father and our Elder Brother. Our union with the Godhead is, therefore, not just an acceptance of right philosophical, or creedal, ritualistic doctrines, but is a close personal union and spiritual bond where we can love and be loved as we give worshipful homage and receive providential blessings. Such a strong, personal union of the worshipper with his God is not possible in other religions, and thus this is a definite plus for Christianity.

In Christianity, the blessings to the Christian are not based upon his merit or slavish "rule keeping" as one "in bondage under law" (see Gal. 4:6-9). Rather they depend upon the merit of Christ as our sin-offering when he shed his blood on the cross (see Rom. 3:25). Salvation is a gift (Eph. 2:8) and is not earned or deserved. This is why Christianity is a grace system, and all of this means that our relationship with our Heavenly Father is based upon a different motivation than mere "reward for good conduct" or "pay for work done." The element of love is dominant, and this motivates the hardened sinner to give up his past life and enter into a new relationship with God's family where sins are forgiven, and adequate motivations flow to induce joyful and holy living in a loving response of faith and trust.

In Christianity we find a uniqueness in that the demand of Christ calls for us to live unselfishly, "in lowliness of mind, each counting other better than himself" (Phil. 2:3). This means that the teachings of Jesus go right down to the bottom of our hearts and root out all of the evil that may lurk there. The Christian's unselfishness, however, is somewhat akin to the meekness mentioned in the Beatitudes — "Blessed are the meek, for they shall inherit the earth" (Matt. 5:5). Marxism and other atheisms ridicule Christianity for teaching meekness, insisting that it denigrates man's own power and makes of him a weakling. That meekness is a superior quality to "might," however, is noticeable in the qualities that we appreciate in our fellow human beings. Never do we appreciate the bully, but considerate and kind gentlemen and women are those whom we appreciate and with whom we prefer to associate.

Christianity's uniqueness is further indicated in that it sponsors a church of a continuing and self-perpetuating group of disciples to carry on its work in the world. It also has a Bible which commands its own loyalty and which can serve as a "testing anvil" for doctrines and philosophies. Unless something is available to guarantee continuing purity of its truth, any movement will collapse in time.

The devotional character and qualities found in the Bible not only make it dear to the Christian heart but give it a quality which enriches and lifts the spiritual life of the worshipper. The sense of being in spiritual union with the Godhead and thus able to interact in personal communion with God is a unique quality not found in other religions. To let one's mind dwell upon God in adoration and worship for a period of time is a wholesome and beneficial experience, especially when one is aware that God is also a person, and is conscious of the worship and appropriately responds.

The total and complete commitment of the Christian in submission to the will of Christ and the understanding that "it is no longer I that live, but Christ liveth in me" (Gal. 2:20), somewhat overwhelms the Christian and gives him a new changed outlook on life. He has a new set of values and finds his joys and happiness measured by a different scale, which to him is higher and more meaningful than the old could ever furnish. In true spiritual meaning he has in fact become "a new creature" (2 Cor. 5:17) — the old man has died (Rom. 6:6), and "the old things have passed away." This is certainly a uniqueness.

CHAPTER 20

BIBLICAL COSMOLOGY

The term cosmology concerns a description of the universe, its organization and meaning. The Greek word "cosmos" means "order," as versus chaos, so there is a strong implication that our universe was considered to be an ordered, well-organized framework, even from the time of the early Greek philosophers. "Order in nature," caused by a divine justice and harmony, is a view that many held long before the time of Christ. Also in the early Greek view is the concept that there is no beginning nor end of time, since it is cyclical, and that there is a set of unalterable laws producing a recurring rhythm in nature and there is thus a permanent and repetitive continuity of events.

By medieval times Christian views had long been held in the western world and the idea of a purposive creation by God had come to be dominant. Miracles and providential activity were considered to be normal, and all fitted into the divine purpose and will.

The New Testament outlook on the world, its origin and arrangement, is colored by figurative language, such as "the four corners of the world," "the sun rising and setting," "heaven as up" and "hell as down," etc., many of which terms we still use, even though we do not take them literally. Certainly the outlook of the early Christians was "pre-scientific" in the modern sense of that term, but it need not be understood to have been as crass and naive as some seem to think today.

To be sure the modern scientific understanding of the physical universe obviates heaven being "up," since the earth is round and rotates daily. All the new knowledge of astronomy, physics, and chemistry with its elements and compounds, requires a new understanding of the physical universe and the interaction of its parts as nature's laws demand. But science's new knowledge is not all that is involved. There is much to be concerned with that science cannot speak about.

Religion and faith ask additional questions. What is the purpose of the universe? What is man, and what are his obligations as he plans and lives his life? What relation does he have to the Creator and the ultimate power in the universe? Is the universe a grand pattern that is working systematically with adequate opportunities for man to "do his thing" properly as time marches on, or is it "a loose process" without purpose and without any meaning to history or the future? Different people have held views similar to all these during this twentieth century, and so it is reasonable for us to look into the problem.

It seems to the present writer that such a well-planned and beautiful universe, with man as the acme of creation, expected to have dominion over all, is not here by chance nor accident, but had to have been created with a purpose and with a goal for man. The biblical account of man's being created in the image of God with free moral choice and moral responsibility seems to fit logically and exactly into all the later biblical teachings, but also into our personal knowledge of the operation of nature and its laws. This means that *there is* a grand pattern and purpose in all things, and that God's person and will are right at the center of it all. There is a universal symmetry that is beautiful to contemplate as we think of design and purpose and a loving mind behind it all.

Among current religious views concerning the cosmology, Liberals feel that modern science has destroyed the cosmology of the Bible, and that therefore it has none of significance. The Neo-Orthodox or existentially oriented religious thinkers feel that there is a meaningful cosmology "between the lines" in the biblical revelation, although they too, do not feel that there is any value in the clearly stated "pre-scientific" statements of the Bible. This so-called "valid" cosmology that is known through "existential awareness," also transcends modern scientific cosmology in their view. They hold for God as Creator and that the creation is subject to God's will, so that there is an ultimate purpose behind it all. Man is the chief creature, is free and responsible, and prone to sin. God's will is, however, known only through a direct confrontation with man and not through the words of scripture. In fact it is a non-communicable knowledge, and could not be stated in words. This makes the whole program highly subjective and it expects that each man will have his own private truth, differing from other people's truths. What God's will is, then, is actually not certainly knowable. It is not an objective, public truth, and the propositional statements of the Bible are thus not dependable for certain knowledge.

The Biblical Cosmology

One should not dare to outline the complete cosmology of the Bible, for sheer reasons of inability. The Bible does, however, give several high points that stand out rather clearly, and they present a quite meaningful view.

The physical universe, with all that we have learned from science, interlocks into one grand system, with chemical and physical laws integrated into a knowable and dependable organization, and the laws of nature carrying on uniformly and regularly in logical relationships.

Behind the physical there lies a spiritual realm of reality which when known gives purpose and meaning and explanation to it all. Man was created in God's image to give glory to Him (Eph. 3:21), and he has free will and moral responsibility. For such a person, who has complete freedom of choice, to worship and love God on his own without any coercion, is for God, who also is a person, to get a real satisfaction from such voluntary love. In the spiritual realm, man must of course choose rightly and must meet his spiritual obligations in order for the Creator to be pleased. Obviously, then, he must someday answer for his choices and be either rewarded or penalized as the case may be. God knew from the start, however, that man would sin, so even from the creation God planned that Jesus should come to earth to seek out and save man through his atoning death on the cross (Rev. 13:8 [note]; 1 Peter 1:20; Gen. 3:15). Sin is repulsive to God, and it is bad enough that its rightful punishment, if unforgiven, is an eternity spent away from God's presence. It is serious enough that it cost the blood of Christ to bring forgiveness, but the love of both God and Christ for man is such that these arrangements were willingly made in order that men could have a hope of redemption from sin.

God works providentially in human lives, and the Holy

Spirit is given to the Christian to live in him for his spiritual benefit. Ultimate victory in life is "guaranteed" to God's children who cling to him in faith (Rom. 8:28); 37-39). Life thus has great meaning and great hope for him who has come to know the Lord in the forgiveness of his sins and has become a member of God's family on earth.

CHAPTER 21

ANTHROPOLOGY OF THE NEW TESTAMENT

Anthropology is technically a study of man. We will limit our concern in this chapter to what the New Testament teaches about the nature of man, his spiritual qualities and relationships.

The apostle Paul speaks of man as "body, soul and spirit" (1 Thess. 5:23). In distinguishing these terms "body" means the material fleshly body; "soul," in this context, means the *animating principle* (such as living animals have and which departs at their death (Eccl. 3:21); and "spirit" means the real inner man, the person, the self, who "returns to God" at death (Eccl. 12:7). The spirit, as the real person, is he who is responsible for the individual's conduct and will answer for it at the last day (2 Cor. 5:10). Death is only a separation of the spirit from the flesh, and the spirit itself has a permanent, continuing existence. As long as the spirit dwells within the body he has the obligation of fighting against the temptations which come through the flesh (Rom. 7:14-25).

Our concern just here is the person's relation to God, which necessarily involves our conduct and response to him in this life, thus the fact of our involvement is sin and its guilt, and whether we can get such guilt removed. A passage of scripture which considers all this in some detail is Romans 7:7-25. We shall here comment upon some of the highlights of this passage as they apply to man's nature and his relationship to God.

In verses 7 through 13 Paul is arguing that man has no guilt for deeds unless there be a law that prohibits the doing of them. For him personally, this was the law of Moses, but in truth it is any law that any person lives under and is obligated to, in whatever age.

Paul was not responsible for his deeds which were done before he reached the age of accountability (v. 9), but when he reached that age he became accountable, and since the law had now become effective he was a guilty sinner, and thus spiritually dead. The law had become that which brought his condemnation and spiritual death, yet the law itself was good and holy, and served a good purpose in God's plan. Paul is here speaking of his own true experience and condition, but these are also valid for every man, whatever law he lives under, and thus in principle this situation is applicable to us today.

In verses 14 through 21 we find somewhat of a "tongue-twisting" passage that is quite bewildering for many people. "I am carnal, sold uner sin," does not mean that one *has to* sin, but that he is subjected to very strong temptations, by reason of his living in the flesh. The inner, spiritual man would really delight in obeying God's law and doing only good things (which indicates how wonderful it will be in heaven when we have no fleshly temptations and we will enjoy worshipping and serving God to the full), but we in truth now find that since we are under the pressure of carnal temptations the inner man winds up losing the battle and being guilty before God. The ultimate source of our final guilt is *Sin* (here personified for *Satan*), and not the deliberate choice or true desire of ourselves. The final outcome, however, is that we do commit wrong deeds and are personally guilty before God. The "law of sin which is in our members" (vv. 21, 22, and 23) is actually the *tendency* to do evil caused by the vary strong pressures which Satan constantly exerts upon us. Man's real trouble is trying to live the good life is that all of us, sooner or later, give in to this tendency (law of sin) and find ourselves "wretched" (v. 24), and greatly in need of deliverance, which must come from someone outside ourselves.

In this passage, then, though we have handled it very briefly, we learn much about man's nature and make-up. He is truly an inner man or spirit being, but he lives in a fleshly body which has carnal appetites, and through these Satan is constantly tempting us and he keeps this "law of sin" operating upon us all the time. The inner man "wars" (v. 23) against this law of sin, the warfare involving "the law of our minds" or God's law that we live under (in whatever age), and in which law we as spirit beings delight (v. 22). Temptation through "the lust of the eye, the lust of the flesh, and the pride of life" (1 John 2:16), ultimately brings all of us "into captivity" (v. 23), and we thus have lost the war and find ourselves in a wretched, hopeless state, unless we can get help from some source outside ourselves.

The blessed hope that man has is in Christ (v. 25), and we find this help detailed in chapter 8 of Romans. In spite of the wretchedness that man is truly in without Christ, "There is no condemnation to them that are in Christ Jesus, because the law of the Spirit of life in Christ Jesus has made (us) free from the law of sin and death" (Rom 8:1, 2). We are freed from the guilt of our past sins, and we also have help and get strength for living our future Christian lives. Triumph is possible through Christ's help, and this is what he came into the world to bring. Those who believe and commit themselves totally to him have no worries — verse 28 guarantees that God "works all things together for good to them that love Him," Adequate spiritual help is furnished therefore to God's true children and victory is assured, in spite of Satan's tempting work and in spite of our human nature. There surely are problems in living life. The non-Christian always remains wretched and without any hope, since hope is possible only through Christ, but the Christian cannot lose, unless he loses his faith!

CHAPTER 22

Anthropology (continued)
HUMAN FREE WILL[31]

When we think of "human free-will" we imply that man, as God's creature, has the power to freely choose both his thoughts and his conduct without any coercion whatever. The opposite doctrine is ordinarily called *determinism,* which means that everything about man's behaviour and thinking has been pre-programmed by the physical cause-effect principles that operate within nature. In this latter case man simply does or thinks what he has to, he has no choice. He is a mere machine or robot.

Probably the majority of philosophers of our day are determinists. Many scientists are. The net influence from these sources in our culture means that a large number of people who are really "laymen" on such topics have been swept up into an acceptance of the doctrine of determinism. For years many argued that "determinism as a basic doctrine has been *proved,*" but Quantum Mechanics and other principles of the "new physics" discovered in this century effectively declared that it is not "proved," although the option may yet be a possibility.

In reply to the arguments favoring determinism, our common sense and the judgments of men throughout history tell us it is not a sound doctrine. Our ordinary human laws take for granted that man can choose, and that he is responsible for his choices. Premeditated murder draws a more severe punishment than accidental killing. People are free to choose whom they shall marry, and they accept responsibility for the choice. Our day to day business dealings are based on free will and responsibility for the consequences of our decisions — our careers, the buying of this or that home, or whether we shall identify with a religious faith — all these are so common that it is not necessary to argue further that men normally believe that man has free will.

---

[31]For a good comprehensive discussion of this topic see W.H. Davis, *The Freewill Question,* The Hague: Martinus Nijhoff, 1971.

The Bible assumes throughout that men are free and responsible. "For freedom did Christ set us free" (Gal. 5:1); "Choose you this day" (Joshua 24:15); "Whosoever will" (Rev. 22:17); "When he knoweth to refuse the evil and choose the good (Isaiah 7:15); and He that believeth and is baptized shall be saved, but he that believeth not shall be condemned" (Mark 16:16).

The entire message of the Bible is built upon the idea that man is made "in the image of God," that he is more than an animal, that he can choose freely to become God's man, or he can choose not to be, but that he will be held reponsible for his choice.

Man is a self-transcendent being. He has the capacity to "stand outside" himself and think about himself, his own weaknesses and strengths. He can evaluate himself, and after consideration and decision he can alter his habits and his character. He is limited by nature as to his physical self and his physical activities, but he has great freedom with respect to his thinking and his commitments. His capacity to "direct" his own thoughts, his actions, and the reformation of his own character may well be confirmation of the idea of "a ghost in the machine," however crude this expression may sound. There surely is a *self* to the human individual that is not a reality for the animal. That the Bible speaks of this as a spirit or an "inward man" is not at all surprising (2 Cor. 4:16; 1 Thess. 5:23)

Another chief distinction about man is the fact that he is a moral being. He has a conscience, a moral awareness, and a sense of "oughtness." There is within him a constant tension between good and evil, right and wrong, and he is expected to make moral decisions, with responsibility for whether they be good or bad. This tension and these decisions are meaningless if he is not free to make choices. If all his thinking and actions are predetermined, he has no responsibility for wrong choices, nor does he have any guilt. The sense of guilt for wrongdoing is very common among men. If he does not have free will this is all meaningless. Certainly it must be admitted that men "think" they have free will and are responsible for their decisions and conduct. No animal has ever exhibited moral awareness nor any guilt feelings. They have no religious inclinations. It should be obvious to thinking people, even though we cannot "prove" with finality that determinism is not true, that man has numerous "internal" qualities that animals do not have.

The intellect enters into human decision, advising the self which alternative is the wiser, but feelings also have an important part in the deciding process. There are numerous reactions that people have which are based on feelings. Whether a sight is "beautiful," whether a choice is "for the good," whether an emotion is "pleasant," are all decided by feelings, and decisions are made on that basis. Of course any decision might be a wrong one, but human beings use both intellect and feelings in making decisions of the will. These feelings are "chosen" by us rather than being programmed into us. When a man makes a decision, he can furnish a reason, based on intellectual judgment and/or feeling as to why he chose that way. He never says, "I couldn't help it."

The possibility of a man reforming his life is obvious from our knowledge of man in the past. It has been done any number of times. And it is done for reasons. The reformation is not forced upon the individual, but it comes from "inside him." We cannot change a man's character against his will. Neither can the "cause-effect" operations of natural law. Man is a responsible self, and he knows that he is responsible. If he makes good choices he profits, but if bad ones, he pays.

Man is a person or self, a spiritual entity, in God's likeness, with complete freedom of choice. God does not suffer Satan to tempt man above his ability to resist (1 Cor. 10:13), neither does he force man as to choices for the good. Man's capacity to worry and to show the emotions of anxiety and joy show that he is not programmed like the animal is, who can only follow his instincts. Animals do not have choices in a real sense but can only do what their type of creature is by nature supposed to do. Man can adapt himself to circumstances and can learn. He is not a mere robot, which is what determinism would require him to be.

Natural law need not be absolute or iron-clad. The God who created all could create natural laws that admit of occasional intervention. The operation of nature can have a general regularity without it having to be an absolute regularity. The determinist is, however, "boxed" in. His view cannot have any flexibility. His arguments must have a universal finality, and nature's laws must have no exceptions, even by the Creator himself.

Other criticisms of determinism are that if it were true, reasoning itself would be useless. My arguments here would have no effect whatever upon learning truth, neither would the arguments that the determinist's use have any value at all. Again, our habits, both good and bad, which we cultivate over a long period of time, are not really the results of our concern and our efforts, but were forced upon us through the programming that we have to give in to. Life is without meaning, and there is no use to make any effort in living. You cannot improve your lot, neither can you do harm to it. You can do no wrong, but neither any right. You are no more than a machine, or a leaf that blows in the wind. Who can believe it?

We still admit that philosophically or scientifically we have no "laboratory proof" that man has free will. But we can say with positiveness that reason and rational thinking show clearly that the good life lived by the man who believes in free will is more logical and reasonable. There are better arguments favoring free will, and the doctrine leads to happier people and people with hope and confidence which the non-believer can never enjoy.

CHAPTER 23

THE PROBLEM OF SUFFERING AND EVIL

Christians and non-Christians alike wonder about the presence of suffering and evil in the world. Why do good people suffer? We might assume that if wicked people suffer, they are being punished for their wickedness. But the facts are that many wicked persons suffer little, while apparently good people suffer much. There is an old proverb that "piety pays, but perversity punishes," but in actual practice this does not seem to hold out.

Philosophers and other prominent thinkers in the world have pondered the why of suffering. This has been done throughout human history, but with no good answer. Some Christians hold that suffering is related to sin, either one's own or someone else's. This may be true but there seemingly is no pattern that can be conceived about it that explains all the various aspects that have to be considered. Some of the problems are: Is there a purpose to suffering? Couldn't a good world have been made without suffering? Why are there wars? Why are there persecutions of special groups or races of peoples? Is there a God up there? Is he really omnipotent? Why doesn't he change all this? Does he care?

We do not have space to go into these questions at length, but we may say that good can come out of suffering. A wholesome attitude toward it is certainly to be desired — self-pity is a terrible thing. We are able to live with suffering, and although it remains a mystery, we can work with it and around it. The world is indeed habitable, and there are many good things about it. We may be babes in a nursery, but God hasn't left any old razor blades around for us to play with. If we adapt to the world as we find it, and "learn to roll with the punches," there is no reason why we cannot get along. And there are many blessings and good things that come with our world and with life. We learn from our experiences and we thus can avoid many pains in the future. Knocks and bumps are therefore educative, and help us to "grow up" and to develop a mature attitude spiritually. The Bible says that "God works all things together for good for those who love him" (Rom. 8:28), and as we develop enough faith we can with confidence transcend most of our daily problems and can live serenely, in spite of our tribulations. This attitude will develop our moral character, so this may well be one of God's purposes in allowing suffering.

Suffering is only one type of evil. Others include the actions of wicked people and such calamities as nature brings, such as earthquakes and floods. Perhaps most evil will ultimately produce some form of suffering, so that suffering and evil are quite closely identifiable.

One reason for there being evil in the world is the fact that it is necessary, in order for human beings to have free will. If all men do have free will, then one evil person may choose to cause suffering to another person. God could not then rush in and stop the action of such a free will, because this would destroy the fact of the free will. Thus evil is necessary in order for us to be human, rather than robots. Men may band together and pass laws against evil actions and may thus reduce the effects of bad choices, but still all evil can never be eliminated. Yet the gain from character building and from the fact that we can by this plan be fully human no doubt offsets the bad effects of the presence of evil.

A chief problem about the presence of evil in the world is probably the one of faith in God. Unbelievers argue that one cannot accept all three of the following statements:

- God is all good.
- God is all powerful.
- Evil is present in our world.

The argument goes like this: If God is all good, he would not want evil and suffering in the world he created. Since suffering is here, God is surely not all powerful, since if he were "all good" he would use his power to eliminate the evil. Thus he cannot be all powerful and all good at the same time and continue to allow evil.

The man who has faith in God's existence, his goodness and his power, does not, however, feel that there is any problem in reconciling these with the presence of evil. We do not know everything, and God may very well have a good reason (as suggested above) for allowing evil in the world. It may be that he has quite good reasons for evil, but we humans do not have that information. There is, therefore, no necessary contradiction in, or problem about the above statements.

Science has made great gains in knowledge in the realm of physical realities (which is the only field in which science can speak with authority), and it can answer questions such as how and when and where, and who, and even what? But science can never answer the question of Why? And there are all kinds of "Why?" questions, as man tries to formulate suitable answers about human existence and the meaning of life.

Free will in a moral universe requires that free moral agents be able to choose either the good or the bad. Logically this is necessary. There could be no world where men with free will would always have to choose the good. This would be a contradiction in terms. They would not be free if they were forced to choose either way.

The book of Job gives the best solution to the dilemma of the presence of evil and suffering that anyone has ever come up with. It is not a neat, rational solution with everything explained. Its conclusion, after a forceful and dramatic presentation of all the angles, is that Job finally realized all that he needed to know — that God is in his heaven, is in full control, that he has a purpose that is being worked out (although Job doesn't know what this purpose is) and that Job should simply, in full faith, continue to believe in God and let him work it out in his own good time. To trust implicitly in the God who is the Creator of it all, is to be able to take tribulations and sufferings in one's stride, and to thus transcend all immediate problems with real confidence and hope.

CHAPTER 24

THE MEANING OF EXISTENCE

Perhaps the greatest question that man has faced during all the ages is, "What is the meaning of human existence?" Humanists, atheists and philosophers who reject the existence of God will say, "There is no meaning!" They have to say this because man himself is the topmost being of the universe in their view, and there is nothing greater than man to plan and order such a thing as purpose in the universe. And, of course, man is pitifully small and helpless in the picture of the total universe, even as we now know it.

Ordinary man, however, cannot accept the answer of these skeptics. To him there must be a meaning in life than transcends what we ordinarily observe in our daily activities. Man's moral responsibility calls for an accounting. Man himself is too great and his potential is too great for him to just fade into nothingness at death. There must be some hope that is not contingent upon human achievements here below, there are so many good people who seemingly "do not have a fair chance" at much accomplishment in life. Surely there must be an after-life when we can have explanations for all the crucial questions that are unexplained during this one.

Indeed, there must be a spiritual realm of reality that does not end with man's physical death — and there are numerous biblical passages which indicate this fact:

2 Corinthians 4:16f — ". . . though our outward man is decaying, yet our inward man is renewed day by day . . . while we look not at the things which are seen, but at the things which are not seen; for the things which are seen are temporal, but the things which are not seen are eternal."

Philippians 1:21 — "For me to live is Christ, and to die is gain."

Galatians 2:20 — "I have been crucified with Christ; and it is no longer I that live, but Christ that liveth in me: and that life which I now live in the flesh I live in faith, the faith which is in the Son of God, who loved me and gave himself for me."

Romans 8:16, 17 — "We are children of God: and if children, then heirs; heirs of God and joint-heirs with Christ; if so be that we suffer with him, that we may also be glorified with him."

There are, of course, any number of other passages in the Bible that teach that this life is not all — in fact, it is only a preparation for the eternal life beyond the grave. So the hope of a good future life is a primary concept of the biblical revelation, and this present life is definitely not final. This, then, gives reason for living a certain quality of life here and now, for the qualifying influence it has for the next life.

But even now, there are still the questions about the purpose and meaning of life. How should it be lived, and why? Unless there is some integrating factor in one's total world view there can be no unifying outlook to give him a sense of something to live for, and which will give to him a purpose and a hope. He needs a vision, such as is reflected in Isaiah 6:1-9. Here the prophet received a vision of the Lord upon his throne, and the scene was almost more than he could cope with. He said: "Woe is me! For I am lost; for I am a man of unclean lips, and I dwell in the midst of a people of unclean lips; for mine eyes have seen the King, the Lord of hosts!" This vision, with its attendant emotions gave to Isaiah an outlook on life that transcended all that he had ever known or thought before. Having seen the Lord, he had a concept that immediately gave meaning and purpose to his life. God *is* in his heaven, and in some way, all is right with the world! If God *is* there, then there is purpose, and a meaning is being worked out — even though we have not previously known what it is, nor do we now know. When a loving Father is definitely in control, we have a basis for trusting that all is well. It is he who gives meaning to the universe and a meaning for human existence. The crucial matter for the ordinary man of every age, then, is to come to have a faith in God, one like Isaiah's, which becomes for him an immediate world view that explains everything and makes everything fall into place.

What can such a vision or faith provide? It says that man is superior to other created beings, is made in God's image and with personal characteristics like him. It says that man is absolutely free as to his moral choices, but that he is responsible for them and must answer for them at the judgment. A "good life" is therefore a requisite for him. There is something to live for, a goal to be attained.

Further inquiry brings love into the picture. It may well be that God, as a person, needed and wanted to love and be loved, and this may have been something to do with his reason for creation. It would not do to create puppets or robots, for forced love would be empty and meaningless. The only other alternative is to hope for love from creatures who were perfectly free to choose whether or not they would love. Thus God made man with a complete freedom of will. But as we noted earlier, this necessarily allows the possibility of bad choices and of evil and suffering in the world. No doubt God receives satisfaction from the love that persons with freedom of choice give to him, but he loved us all abundantly even before we loved him in return. So we too are blessed overwhelmingly in this arrangement. Knowing that we would sin before he created us, he planned that the Christ would give his own life on the cross for us that redemption from our sins would be possible. In this way ultimate, final, and absolute victory will belong to those who believe in a totally-committed sense.

There is, then, a meaning and a purpose in life for the ordinary man. There is reason for his having been created and for his existence upon the earth. As he walks across the stage of action of his "threescore years and ten" he has choices — either to live for God and in God's way, or to live for self and futility. Faith in Christ, with its demands of trust and commitment, leading to the presentation of "our bodies as living sacrifices" is the central hope of humanity and the focal reason for our existence. It brings us an ordered and loving life, with abundant joys and the best possible happiness for the here and now, because it is constantly pointing us to the right world-view, that of the vision of Jehovah God in his heaven and all the universe under his direct control and working toward a fulfillment of his specific plan.

To illustrate, one of the highpoints about being a Christian is that we experience a new birth, spiritually, and in fact become "new creatures." This is a reality that is not conceived by the non-Christian and is somewhat beyond his comprehension. But in our spirit-realm existence the change does occur, and we are adopted as God's own children and heirs. We can call the Father "Abba" or *"Daddy"* in the close and intimate way that a small child does it in ordinary human experience. As new creatures, we have figuratively been "changed from pigs into sheep," and no longer do we desire to "wallow in sin," as before. Our spiritual nature has been changed through the process that made us Christians.

CHAPTER 25

THE CHRISTIAN MORAL STANDARD

Two great questions that concern people of today are: "Why be good?" and its corollary, "What is goodness, anyway, and how is it determined?"

Man was created with a moral conscience, which comes into its maturity about the age of puberty. He has a sense of "oughtness," and all men are well-aware of this. We ought to do good, else our conscience will trouble us. This in no way tells us what the good thing is, but it simply insists that we do what we believe at the time to be good. Paul, when he persecuted Christians before his conversion, had a good conscience (Acts 23:1), since he was doing what he thought to be right. Yet he was not right, as he later realized. So one's conscience is simply that inborn urge to do what one understands at the time to be right, but it does not furnish the correct information as to what is truly right and wrong. Our "education" on these matters must come from elsewhere. But all men have a conscience. Some get it "seared over" by doing wrong so much that it no longer bothers them to do wrong. It is a sin to violate one's conscience (Rom. 14:23) — to go against that inborn urge deliberately, so the real reason *why* one should be good is because it is right and is in keeping with the nature that God gave us.

This leaves us with the question of how to know the difference between good and bad, between right and wrong, and in the light of recent experience in America this is no·small problem. Frankly, there is an answer, but it is a biblical answer, and most people in our culture refuse to face this. They still find themselves bewildered and confused, however, and they are unable to decide what is right and what is wrong, as far as a public moral standard is concerned. Our Supreme Court, for example, does not know how to define pornography, and although they would be willing to declare it "out of bounds" if they could, to define it exactly calls for a value judgment, and value judgments are beyond precise description by their very nature.

This last fact is true because there are two realms of reality

— "things seen" and "things unseen" (2 Cor. 4:18). The physical world of things seen is the realm of reality where all things can not only be seen but they can be touched, weighed, divided, and measured. They all consist of *matter* and thus are subject to description by scientists. Our knowledge in this realm is "public" or objective knowledge, knowable by all men alike.

On the other hand the other realm is that of values, spirit, and abstract entities, none of which are "seeable" with any of our five senses. Knowledge here cannot be public because it is non-descriptive. Each person knows it for himself, but he cannot *describe it* to another. For instance, one cannot describe exactly such things as a fighting heart, why one thing is more beautiful than another thing, what goodness is, and so on. The morals problem fits in here. By ordinary human philosophy there thus can be no public moral standard. All we can have is at the level of human opinion, and we have to say that one man's opinion has to be equal to another's. This is why, unless we accept divine revelation, man never has, nor can he, arrive at a public moral standard, or any other public truth in the value realm.

To glance at the history of human thought for illustration of the impossibility of human philosophy to find public truth in the moral or value realm, we recall that the Greek Sophists before Plato's day had decided and were teaching that there is no such thing as public truth of any kind. Plato, who realized that no society could endure if it did not have some kind of an agreed-upon moral standard, argued that there is a public truth in morals. He was forceful enough to capture popular support and to win the day by his personal dominance, but his arguments were later found to be deficient. He claimed that moral judgments were simply a matter of education. When one studies them adequately he will know the public truth. Plato was then naive enough to think that all men would be glad to do good as soon as they learn what it is, but he really did not understand human nature on this point. Aristotle also held, with his teacher Plato, that public truth is knowable in the moral realm, but he believed that it was to be determined by trial and error. It is located in between the extremes of excess and vice — what we might call the happy medium, or what he called "the golden mean." This too, proves to be a naive solution, because people cannot agree on where the golden mean lies. Epicurus came next with his philosophy that the good is "what gives pleasure." Though he personally was somewhat ascetic, his views have been carried to the extreme of a radical pleasure-seeking hedonism. A weakness here is that what gives pleasure tonight may also give a "dark brown hangover" tomorrow. Stoic thinkers who are next, argued that it is futile to worry about morals, since our lives are completely determined and we cannot change them, even if we should want to. We have no choice nor free will in our thinking.

In the modern period the Utilitarian philosophers "came again" with the pleasure principle, but their's was "democratic." A thing is "good" if it gives a pleasure to a large number of people, even though it may cause pain to one or a few. This also proves to be an unsatisfactory explanation, and somehow it shows the continuing distress of men trying to find out by mere speculative human philosophy the difference between goodness and badness. In our own century, Existentialism has declared again with the Sophists that there is no public truth, and of course this applies to morality. They are joined by other prominent philosophies that have flowered in this twentieth century, as Pragmatism, Logical Positivism, and Phenomenology. All of these deny that there is a public moral standard or truth, and since in total they have numerous followers, this one idea proves to be a main cause behind our moral malaise of the current age. We today are in a period of sexual revolution, where homosexuality, extramarital relations, living together without benefit of a marriage commitment, and other similar expressions are practically considered to be "good" and, indeed, the norm. Greed and covetousness have captured many of our politicians, and any number of other deviations from former standards accepted in our society are today rampant. There has clearly been a change, and it is primarily based upon the wrong philosophy — both as to what is real, and as to how true knowledge comes to us.

In the light of human experience, shown in the above brief

history, it is obvious that agreement never can be reached wherein an absolute standard of morals can be derived, if we limit ourselves to speculative human reasoning.

If we will be willing to admit of revelation from the God who made us and *knows* us — even to the number of hairs on our heads and to the thoughts and intents of our hearts — knows our temptations and weaknesses as well as our capacities, we can find an objective, public, yea even an absolute, standard of morality from his revelation, and which in a practical way could serve for all our needs. Our lives would be better, happier, more definite and we could more easily realize how to live the good life.

As an illustration, God has declared some attitudes and practices to be unequivocally *wrong* — "Do you not know that the unrighteous will not inherit the kingdom of God? Do not be deceived; neither the immoral, nor idolaters, nor adulterers, nor homosexuals, nor thieves, nor the greedy, nor drunkards, nor revilers, nor robbers will inherit the kingdom of God" (1 Cor. 6:9, 10). If we are able to believe in God and that he has revealed his will to us, then it is no trouble for us to accept his teachings as setting definite and absolute standards for human conduct. For *good* attitudes and conduct, the following illustration is noteworthy — "Finally, brethren, whatever is true, whatever is honorable, whatever is just, whatever is pure, whatever is lovely, whatever is gracious, if there is any excellence, if there is anything worthy of praise, think about these things" (Phil. 4:8).

The beautiful Sermon on the Mount (Matt. 5, 6 and 7) is considered even by biblical critics to be the best ethical treatise known to man. It consists not in just a collection of good proverbs, but in setting forth ethical principles that endure, and that fit men of all ages. The scriptures in their total ethical pronouncements therefore furnish the best possible information on why be good? and on what goodness is — primarily because they tell us how to be rightly related to our heavenly Father. The vision of him as real and as giving us teachings to guide us aright in our attitudes and conduct make us see that his will for us can be the true absolute public moral standard, and that this is the only way that we can ever have it. His ethics are adapted to our natures exactly, and obviously they expect from us the very highest in behaviour and conduct. Nothing petty or shameful is tolerated. Precise demands as to sexual behaviour and the other strong temptations that men meet are explicitly laid out and there is no reason for the serious Christian to misunderstand about how to live rightly.

CHAPTER 26

CHRISTIAN MORALITY APPLIED

In this chapter we touch only briefly on a few of the major moral problems of the present day. We cannot do a thorough study, and thus will only indicate some of the basic biblical teachings that should be applied to these problems.

Marriage and Sex

In the beginning God ordained marriage for the union of a man and a woman. It was to be for life. Sex within marriage is proper and holy, and it can be beautiful. It contributes meaningfully to the union. It is, however, never to be engaged in outside of marriage. Immorality (fornication), adultery and homosexuality are all condemned in no uncertain terms (1 Cor. 6:9-11), and it is a sad commentary on a society (such as ours today) that attempts to dignify such practices and to declare them moral and socially acceptable.

Most all societies in the past have recognized with hesitancy that harlotry and its kindred vices were wrong and were not to be practiced. The Bible goes further by spelling it out, that "they who practice such things cannot inherit the kingdom of God" (v. 10).

A man is to leave his father and his mother and cleave unto his wife, and the two shall become one flesh. What God has thus joined together, no man is to put asunder. Further, no third party is ever to invade the relationship.

Homosexuality

The practice of homosexual eroticism, which has been clamoring for dignity in recent years in our culture, is abhorred by God (Rom. 1:26-32). This is true to the point that the Bible says that "they who practice such things deserve to die (the second death)" Of course any person who has homosexual feelings that he cannot help, and who never practices such relations, does not sin. But authorities says that in all but a very few cases this is a "learned attitude" and that what is learned can be unlearned. The problem is that many do not want to unlearn it or "cure" their problem, but rather wish to continue practicing it. For these we urge another look at God's will. There are, of course, sinful heterosexual relationships, as we have been warning against, and so there are many people who get themselves into unions and relationships where there can be no sure hope of living "well-pleasing unto God" except to live completely celibate for the rest of their days. This is considered to be a big price to pay, but eternity is forever, and if this is a person's true condition, no price is too big for the hope of heaven.

Celibacy

The practice of complete sexual sublimation or living in celibacy can be spiritually wholesome — provided one has the power of continence and can be happy in this type of life (1 Cor. 7:1-9). But where people do not have such an adequate self-control, "to avoid fornication" (any illicit sex relationship), they are to get married (v. 9) "for it is better to marry than to lust."

Proscriptions against marriage "for the clergy" as a group therefore proves to be a bad regulation, since no entire group would likely have all its members fully continent, and the likelihood of their being tempted above their endurance poses a real problem. To therefore deny the privilege of marriage "to the clergy" as a church requirement is not God's teaching but has some other source. It probably produces more harm than is realized.

Abortion

A very serious practice has developed recently in America, where the abortion of an infant from the womb of its mother is declared to be legal "if the mother does not want the child!" The argument goes that "It's my body, and only I have the right to say what I do with my own body." Normally we would agree with this logic, except for the fact that we are not dealing with just the mother's body. We are dealing with the life of another human being, and the rights of the child to his own life are just as important in fact as the rights of the mother, since the decision is not just about one person but two. The logic of the abortionists would hold that the fetus is no more important than the afterbirth — at least if the abortion is early enough in the pregnancy.

Some biblical statements indicate with certainty the fact of the personhood of the human embryo:

Eccl. 11:5 — As you do not know how the spirit comes to the bones in the womb of a woman with child, so you do not know the work of God who makes everything.

Luke 1:15 — (Speaking of John the Baptist before his birth) ". . . he will be filled with the Holy Spirit, even from (Gk. *ek,* out of) his mother's womb . . ."

Luke 1:41-44 — (Speaking of John as an embryo) "And when Elizabeth heard the greeting of Mary, the babe leaped in her womb; and Elizabeth was filled with the Holy Spirit . . . For behold, when the voice of your greeting came to my ears, the babe in my womb leaped for joy." (Would this leap for joy have been possible if the embryo was a non-person and only a glob of matter?)

Jesus, who preexisted (Phil. 2:6-8) then became man through being an embryo in the womb of Mary, was obviously as person during the entire time of the pregnancy.

What human, be he legislator or judge, can state at what instant the spirit of a human enters an embryo? Who is to say that "only after six months is the embryo a person, and it would not be murder to abort before that time?" Every indication is that life and personhood is present from the instant of conception.

CHAPTER 27

THE PLACE OF THE NEW TESTAMENT

One of the reasons given by some scholars for Christianity being able to drive out its competitors in the early period of the Christian era is that it had a Bible and a church. These competitors for the loyalties of men at that time were pagan philosophy, especially Stoicism, and the competing religions, including the fertility cults, the Emperor worship cult, and the mystery religions. The place of and the need for a "Bible" by a growing and expanding religious movement is obvious. It served for an authority in cases of problems and/or misunderstanding. It served as teaching material, since a knowledge of the religion is necessary for growth.

The Bible has always been the world's most studied book. The Old Testament is the first book ever translated from one language into another — Hebrew to Greek about 275 B.C. This was to serve people whose language was changing to Greek due to the conquests of Alexander the Greet and the cultural changes in his empire. The basic demand of the Bible itself is that it be studied and known. A limited knowledge of it is necessary to becoming "a child of God" and a growing, continuing knowledge of its principles is the expected thing for the normal Christian.

The really important thing about the New Testament as we contemplate the impact of Christianity is that it is that which made Christianity what it is. It is the book of teaching, for both principles and details; it is the book of reference for settling questionable problems; its teachings set forth the actual will of God for man and the diligent student knows that these writings are of such spiritual quality and depth that they could not have been written by uninspired men.

The religious system unfolded in the pages of the New Testament is, strangely enough, not what many people in our American culture of today would expect. New Testament Christianity is not denominational — in the sense that groups with a strong internal distinctiveness band together, but tolerate other groups as also being equally in the sheep-fold. Jesus prayed

(John 17) that his followers be one. He himself founded and built the New Testament church (Matt. 16:18f) and nowhere in the Bible can his church be considered as only a part of the whole of God's people. The church that Christ built is itself "the body of Christ" and therefore is the kingdom of God on earth. God himself adds all the saved to this body (Acts 2:47), and nowhere can we get any biblical support for Christ's church being denominational in any sense at all. We must conclude that denominational concepts are only human and are not biblical.

The above being true, the Lord's church is doctrinally neither Liberal, Evangelical, Catholic, nor Fundamentalist. It is biblical! It is philosophically neither realist nor idealist. It partakes of both objective realities (facts), and subjective concepts (faith) but it is radical in neither.

There is no doubt some truth in all philosophies and ideologies, some truth in all religious doctrinal programs, but the New Testament religion with Jesus Christ as its Lord and Savior is distinct from all philosophies and theologies of human origin and which at best have only a limited portion of truth. It has it all!

Basic Christianity, that is supported at every point by New Testament authority, has all the truth and none of the error of other religions or of denominational groups that consider themselves to be Christian. No distinctive doctrine of any religious group that is peculiar to them can be found in the New Testament.

All these thoughts should point each of us to soul-searching and to Bible-searching, to learn the origin and authority for our own doctrinal views, and indeed our relation to the New Testament's teachings. It alone is God's revelation, and it warns us against doctrines of men (Matt. 15:8, 9; 2 John 9; Rom. 16:17).

CHAPTER 28

THE THEOLOGY OF THE NEW TESTAMENT

The term "theology" comes from the Greek words "theos," God, and "logos," word or study. Technically it means the overall view of doctrine or teaching that anyone holds or, in this case, that the New Testament sets forth. It compares to "philosophy" or "world view" in the broad sense of one's outlook, but it definitely accepts the idea of the existence and dominance of God in the universe, and the fact that he has revealed himself to man in some manner. All the major religious systems have a theology of some sort, but we here limit our concern to the overall major doctrinal system that the New Testament sets forth.

We have already suggested numerous points about the New Testament theology in the previous chapters on Cosmology and on Internal Evidences, where we discussed the Unity of the Bible, the relation of the Testaments and the place of the Old Testament for today's study. We begin here then with additional and sharper concerns to these as we probe the details of Christianity as a religious system and further into its overall thrust.

One very important matter about which there has been controversy is whether the Bible is a "pattern" revelation — that is, is it a blueprint to be followed exactly in relating one-self to God, or can it be superseded by feelings or subjective inti-mations, or even by some "authoritative spokesman" such as a priest? In other words, how should we look at the Bible? Must we take its "chapter and verse" demands at face value or can we explain them away in favor of something we like better? In Matthew 15:8, 9 Jesus warns us pointedly about "teaching as doctrines the precepts of men;" and in Matthew 7:21-24 he explicitly states that only by doing the Lord's will in contrast to our own ideas, can we have any hope of entering into heaven. There are any number of passages warning against false teachers (See 2 John 2:9; Titus 1:9-11; Rom. 16:17).

That Christianity is a "system" of teachings, organized into a pattern program of religious worship and service, is discussed quite fully in this author's *Heaven's Window*,[29] but here we content ourselves with some passages in the New Testament itself which make the specific claim:

> *Romans 6:17* - "You . . . have become obedient from the heart to the standard (Greek *tupon*) of teaching to which you were committed . . ." This word *tupon* means type, mould, or norm, and suggests that the teaching shapes and moulds our lives and conduct. This, then, shows that the teaching of the New Testament is the *norm* or pattern to which we should align ourselves.

> *2 Timothy 1:13* - "Follow the pattern (*hupotuposin*) of sound words which you have heard from me." This word is related to *tupon* and is defined as model, standard, determinative example, and so makes it unequivocal that the New Testament is to be our pattern.

> *Hebrews 8:5* - "They serve as a copy (*hupodeigmati*) and shadow of the heavenly sanctuary; for when Moses was about to erect the tent, he was instructed by God, saying 'See that you make everything according to the pattern (*tupon*) which was shown you in the mountain.'" The definition of *hupodeigma* is given as model, example, image, and as something that does or should spur one on to imitate it.

Additional passages, should we need them, include: 2 Thessalonians 3:6; 1 Corinthians 4:6; Galatians 1:6-8; Ephesians 4:14 and Romans 10:17.

When we think of the Christian religion as carrying pattern obligations upon the believer, we realize that this includes the things needed to become a Christian, or what we may ordinarily call the plan of salvation. Since in principle the Christian's life is to be completely surrendered to God's service, this can only be done by obedience to the detailed commandments of New Testament teaching. Human doctrines, plans, and ideas of what "seems right" must be forgotten and God's revealed will must be meticulously followed, else one would not be totally yielded. Not only then, the requirements of the plan of salvation that brings one into the family of God, but also the

---

[29]Abilene: Biblical Research Press, 1974, pp. 72-106.

appointments of worship, the manner of church organization, and other similar matters should follow the scriptures carefully. After all, intellectual correctness is a necessity in all areas of human endeavor. Ignorance does not produce desired results and in today's world it is counted as intolerable. The surgeon must know his exact problem and its exact solution, or else there is disaster. So it is with God's will. Christianity is concerned with the whole of man and with the whole of truth. God wishes man to develop spiritually into a magnificent character with godlikeness. Such cannot be brought about by a vague subjectivity or by some idealism that never touches base with hard reality. God's revelation must be considered and respected as his revelation, and we should be as careful with it as with the wording of a law in a court of litigation.

The Faith-Works Problem

The justifying principle under the law of Moses was works, or "exact obedience." The law was to be obeyed, which is really all that one can do with law. Obey and be blessed, or disobey and be condemned! There is no mercy or forgiveness possible in a merely legal program; there is no Saviour to help or save. It all depends upon one's own good deeds and his own merit. Justification would be granted as a debt owed him, because he has earned his reward.

On the contrary, the principle of justification under the teachings of Christ is *grace,* where the final reward or destiny is based, not upon one's deserving but upon the merit of the Saviour who died on the cross, and the salvation is given as a gift to the person who qualifies by having a saving and trusting *faith.* Under grace there is no human merit or earning power — this resides in the atoning power of Christ — and the human sinner is justified as a gift, because of the love of God and Christ for him, and of course, because he is now trusting in Christ completely.

The problem of faith and works and their interrelationship is probably the strongest problem of interpretation that has faced the church in its two thousand years of history. It surely is the cause of much denominationalism that we find today.

Specifically, some claim that salvation in Christ is conditioned upon "faith only" — that is, no *work* whatever, no deeds, no actions or expressions of the faith are necessary for one to be forgiven of his sins and inducted into the family of God. These people have a famous passage that they quote — "For God so loved the world that he gave his only son, that whoever *believes* in him should not perish, but have eternal life" (John 3:16). Also there are other passages that lend support to this in their view —

Ephesians 2:8-10 - "For by grace have ye been saved through faith, and that not of yourselves, it is the gift of God; not of works, that no man should glory."

John 3:36 - "He that believeth on the son hath eternal life."

1 John 5:1 - "Whosoever believeth that Jesus is the Christ is begotten of God."

Acts 16:31 - "Believe on the Lord Jesus, and thou shalt be saved and thy house."

In the consideration of only the above scriptures it could be easy to see why these people can accept the idea that no work or activity enters into the plan of salvation. They decide that it boils down to a simple change in one's mental attitude or a decision that one can make to give mental assent to a certain statement, and that such is the only condition at all that must ever be met in order to claim God's full and complete salvation in Christ.

On the other hand, however, there are other passages that can be arrayed that indicate that obedience to God's will (to his commands), that repentance, that love and a complete commitment to Christ's will must be complied with. And further, that even an obligation to live a godly life and to grow in grace must be assumed and faithfully attempted. Such passages include:

Matthew 7:21 - "Not everyone that saith unto me, Lord, Lord, shall enter into the kingdom of heaven, but he that doeth the will of my father who is in heaven."

Romans 2:6 - "In the day of wrath and revelation the righteous judgment of God, who will render to every man according to his works."

> Revelation 22:12 - "Behold, I come quickly, and my reward is with me, to render to each man according to his works."

> James 2:24 - "Ye see that by works a man is justified, and not only by faith."

When these latter passages are considered it is easy to see that their meaning contradicts the conclusion drawn about the first group, as noted above. Surely a correct interpretation is not to assume that the Bible is clearly contradictory of itself, but it is to seek out a harmony of these passages that will stand the full tests of scholarly investigation.

The dilemma may further be heightened by looking at Paul's Romans 4:5 statement,

> "And Abraham believed God, and it was reckoned unto him for righteousness. Now to him that worketh, the reward is not reckoned as of grace, but as of debt. But to him that worketh not but believeth on him that justifieth the ungodly, his faith is counted for righteousness."

And then comparing it with James' dictum,

> "Was not Abraham our father justified by works, in that he offered up Isaac his son upon the altar? Thou seest that faith wrought with his works, and by works was faith made perfect; and the scripture was fulfilled which saith, 'and Abraham believed God and it was counted unto him for righteousness'" (James 2:21-23).

The solution to the seeming discrepancy between these two passages is to understand that words have more than one meaning. Most words have several meanings, and the words "faith" and "works" which are the focus of our concern here certainly do this. We shall study two major meanings of each, all of which are clearly indicated in the Greek lexicons as valid meanings in appropriate contexts:

Faith (#1)—This is the limited or narrow meaning of the word and simply means "the mental assent to a propositional statement." One reaches a mental decision and says, "Yes I accept that as a true statement," and he has exhausted this limited meaning. Examples from scripture of this meaning are:

James 2:19 - "Even the demons believe and shudder."

John 12:42 - "Nevertheless many even of the authorities believed in him, but for fear of the Pharisees they did not confess it, lest they should be put out of the synagogue."

No salvation is possible with such a limited, narrow faith. Yet people today are teaching "salvation by faith only" with no more understanding than to believe that this is the sort of faith that saves.

Faith (#2)—This is a broader meaning, quite comprehensive, and includes all that a man must do to be saved. It of course begins with the intellectual assent of accepting the truth of the statement that Jesus is the Christ, the Son of the living God. But more — this faith includes repentance, love, trust, complete commitment and, yea, even obedience to Christ's will. This "saving faith" is a complete delivery of self in submission to the will of Christ and has the attitude of "Speak, Lord, thy servant heareth, command and I will obey." It is more than mere mental assent. It requires a life to be lived in yielded submission.

Our solution to the interpretation problem is that when the Bible says that we are saved by faith, it means this complete, total, comprehensive faith. The demons and the authorities had a "faith" but it did not lead them to love, trust, repent or obey, and it did not save them.

Works (#1—"Works" here means the works "done for pay" as under the law of Moses (Phil. 3:9), where human merit and deserving is the consideration for justification, and which, of course, no human ever met ("All have sinned and fall short"— Rom. 3:23).

Works (#2)—This is the "obedience of faith" in the Christian grace system where there is no human merit involved but where the work is done because of love and our relationship to Christ. There is a desire to yield one's self and to obey Christ's commandments because of the gratitude that we feel for his and the Father's love for us. The idea of being a part of the spiritual family of the great Creator God is all the motive needed for obedience, and one rejoices at the privilege.

Saving faith, then is obviously the broader, comprehensive meaning, and the motivation for the Christian's works is love, not pay. Yet the Christian has to obey! Should he refuse, or fail to obey in the face of Christ's commands, we would have to say that he really did not love the Lord enough for his faith to be the saving variety. The Christian should both teach and practice obedience, as a matter of making his faith "perfect," but never for the purpose of trying to earn his way to heaven. We are "not under law, but under grace," and our works are not done for the purpose of merely complying with the requirements of a legal system, they are done out of gratitude and love as natural responses to God's love and grace. We must keep in mind the distinction between the two great covenants of the Bible, and that the principles of justification in each are different from the other. The types and motivations of the obedience in the two are entirely different things, and we cannot interpret the Bible correctly if we confuse the two. If seems to be easy for some people to decide that since we are "not justified by the works of the law" (Gal. 2:16), that no work whatever is bound upon us — not even good works (see Eph. 2:10). On the other hand, there are some who understand clearly that the Christian must be an obedient Christian, but think of the Christian system as just another mere law, in the same sense that the law of Moses was a mere law. These latter do not comprehend well enough the fact of the cross as our sin atonement, of our need of a Saviour, and of the real meaning of God's grace.[30] The happy medium between both of these distorted understandings is to see that faith is the saving principle in the grace program, but it is not real faith unless it is an obedient faith.

---

[30]See this author's, *The Biblical Doctrine of Grace,* Abilene: Biblical Research Press, 1977

CONCLUDING
OBSERVATIONS

CHAPTER 29

SOUL WINNING

In view of God's many gracious provisions for his believing children, all motivated by his great love for us, and even more by his love for all mankind, it is no wonder that he expects us to individually be soul winners. The Great Commission, well expressed by Matthew (28:18-20) charges every baptized believer to "make disciples of all nations, baptizing them into the name of the Father and the Son and the Holy Spirit, teaching them to do all things I have commanded you." This solemn charge and responsibility is most natural, since the truly converted person can see the importance of saving other souls who can also freely share in these same great spiritual blessings. His heart will be filled with love for Christ, and for those whom Christ loves enough to die for, and in the face of this he will be positively active in passing on the saving message.

This present life is for each of us important enough that we want to make the most of it, and to live as long as we may. But in view of eternity and the spiritual relationships that the Christian has, he realizes that the number-one consideration in all of the earth life is to be rightly related to God and to the sacrificial atonement of Jesus Christ on the cross. This relationship requires that we count spiritual values as coming first, and that an integral part of proper spiritual values is for each of us to be "ministers of the word" to others, both by mouth and by the example of our lives. It means that if we earn our living by some other vocation than "preaching," we have the obligation and privilege of giving our money as well as our time, our talents and our interests to the spreading of the gospel message of salvation. We are committed to living for Christ, so his will continues to be the first consideration of our lives. We feel this responsibility and are glad to discharge it as individuals, without the necessity of or the pressure of ecclesiastical demands. Even though the Lord's church has no earthly headquarters or denominational machinery, individual Christians carry out his will faithfully because of their personal relationship to him and their knowledge of his will.

CHAPTER 30

DEPTH SPIRITUALITY

In Galatians 6:1 we read "ye who are spiritual should restore him (the person overcome by a wrong) in a spirit of gentleness." The suggestion that certain Christians can be truly "spiritual" is intriguing. This certainly is the ideal for Christians to seek after — to be spiritually minded and filled with spiritual understanding and appreciation. But so many people in the world have a long way to go before they can reach that plateau. What is the nature of spiritual maturity and how can it be attained.?

In Colossians 1:9, 10 we find a similar reading to the one above — ". . . we have not ceased to pray for you, asking that you may be filled with the knowledge of his will in all spiritual wisdom and understanding, to lead a life worthy of the Lord, fully pleasing to him, bearing fruit in every good work and increasing in the knowledge of God." Here again is mentioned the possibility of spiritual growth and development. It is based, for one thing, on a knowledge of God and of his will. This is one reason that non-Christians can have no real spiritual depth or appreciation — because of their ignorance of God's will. This lack of knowledge is no doubt based upon the presupposition prevalent in our culture that the Bible is not God's will and that, although it is a good book, it is not really all that important. But depth spirituality, which is an ideal to be striven after in this life, is impossible without a depth knowledge of God and this can be had only by a serious study of his word.

The antonym for spirituality is carnality. "To be carnally minded is death, but to be spiritually minded is life and peace" (Rom. 8:6). Spirituality and carnality are discussed as opposites in 1 Corinthians 2:13-3:1, so if we can determine a clear meaning of carnality we can better sense the meaning of spirituality. "Carnal" means "of the flesh, fleshly" but this basically means not flesh as in meat, but as in fleshly appetites, the gratification of which merely satisfies the physical body. Satan tempts us through our fleshly appetites as indicated in 1 John 2:16 (see Chapter 22), so a strong interest in carnality or things which gratify the flesh works against our spiritual well-being and our approvedness of God. To be carnally minded is to have an interest only in the baser things that come our way. These carnal interests are cultivated by the philosophy that says that each of us is his own moral authority, and when we accept this view we obviously choose those ways of life that titillate and gratify our desires. There is no place for spiritual appreciation in such an attitude, for there is apt to be no knowledge of or concern for God to base it on.

A true "depth spirituality" can be achieved only by one who learns of God and Christ and of God's plans and purposes as outlined in his plan of redemption found in the scriptures. One catches a glimpse of God's love for sinful man and this sparks a love on our part for him in return. The story of the cross and the love there expressed appeals to all except the most hard-hearted, and we are encouraged to commit our lives in faith to Christ. Almost every line of the Bible expresses a note of cheer and love and hope.

> The steadfast love of the Lord never ceases,
>   his mercies never come to an end;
> they are new every morning;
>   great is thy faithfulness.
> "The Lord is my portion," says my soul,
>   "therefore will I hope in him."
>   —Lamentations 3:22-24

It is sad that many Christians, after baptism into Christ (Gal. 3:27), do not continue to seriously study God's will, and therefore do not continue to grow in spirituality. They cheat themselves out of much of the beauty and joy that goes with the Christian life, when lived at its best. It is further sad that some church leaders, who may have been selected only on the basis of personality and popularity, do not do much study, looking toward a high degree of spiritual discernment in the future. We fear that many, upon selection to a church office, feel that their present state of biblical knowledge is "terminal," and since they knew enough to be appointed, they have no need to grow more. Such leaders often tend to settle for a mechanical understanding of the demands of Christianity, and feel that to keep the

minimum commandments is enough and that God will "punci.
our tickets" into heaven on the basis of our own goodness. This
attitude is mere legalism, and fails to show a proper respect for
Christ's atoning death. Jesus did not die in order to give us a
good set of rules whereby we can save ourselves. He died to
make it possible for God to forgive us "freely" by our trusting in
and depending on the power of his shed blood. To try to earn
our own right to live in heaven is to ignore and reject what Jesus
did for us, yea, it is to say that he died a useless death. Such an
attitude is a long way from saving faith. In fact, it is totally
unspiritual. The law of Moses was that kind of a set of rules, and
it could save no one. That is why it had to be replaced by the
Christian *grace* program. Real spirituality realizes that God has
done great things for us, and it shows love and gratitude to him
for it.

Depth spirituality is adapted to man's high capabilities.
Whereas man has the inherent capacities of love, worship,
appreciation of the good, resistance to wrong and similar characteristics that show him to be above animals and actually a
potential partaker of the divine nature, the things of the Spirit
appeal to him and can be appreciated by him. It is possible for
man to "set his mind on things of the Spirit" (Rom. 8:8) and for
him to "walk not according to the flesh but according to the
Spirit" (v. 4; also see Gal. 5:16). He is capable of "bearing the
fruit of the Spirit" in his life, such things as "love, joy, peace,
patience, kindness, goodness, faithfulness, gentleness, and self
control" (Gal. 5:22, 23). These capabilities are not available to
mere animals and this fact reveals that man is truly made in
God's image; but neither are they available to carnally minded
man, who has the capability but not the will. He does not wish
to be spiritual and is content simply to gratify the lusts of the
flesh.

The spiritual person who in full faith commits himself and
his will completely unto God will come to have "the peace of
God, which passes all understanding . . ." (Phil. 4:7), and can
thus have a calm and serene life filled with hope and confidence. Much of his religious knowledge is based upon his use of
reason (1 Pet. 3:15), but ultimately his faith transcends that

which he can see and personally experience (Heb. 11:1), and in fact "passes understanding" — goes beyond what he can logically and rationally analyze and comprehend. At this point his sense of peace and of the well-being of his soul means ultimate happiness, yet it is grounded upon his "squaring" with all that he possibly can know of God's will and his way through a reasoned understanding of his revelation and his own experience of life. He is truly peaceful.

The Christian's acceptance by God and his own confidence and hope that it is a reality is not based upon his own intellect, education, or super-wisdom of any sort. It is available to the normal person who is old enough to have reached the age of accountability and who has what we might call normal mental faculties. The "plain man" thus can enjoy God's approval just as can the intellectual. Because of the possibility of the sin of pride, he might even have a better chance for divine approvedness. The quantity of religious knowledge needed to obey the gospel (2 Thess. 1:8) and become a Christian, and then to live a life well-pleasing unto God, does not require great intellect or a great education, although it does require some exercise of the intellect and an acceptance of the preached word (Rom. 10:17). Any normal person who is accountable can fully bask in God's approval provided he has the right attitude and is willing to grow in grace.

The yoke of Jesus is easy, and his burden is light (Matt. 11:30), so it is not difficult to go to heaven for the person with a saving faith. His hope is based upon reasoning and logic, as they are applied to the teachings of the scriptures, and as one grows in his spiritual discernment and appreciation they fall into place and "make good sense." His hope is meaningful in that it answers the problems that he feels about himself, his temptations and his need for explanations about life. We couldn't know why, rationally, that God should send his own son to die for our sins, and if we had been trying to figure out a religion for man we would never have thought of this. But it works! It is the very message that appeals to sinful man and brings him to repentance. God was wise! He knew!

CHAPTER 31

SPIRITUAL POWER

There is such a reality as spiritual power — "my speech and my preaching were not in words of wisdom but in demonstration of the Spirit and of power; that your faith should not stand in the wisdom of men but in the power of God" (1 Cor. 2:4, 5). This power is available to the Christian to aid him in living the Christian life. It is found, in one way, in the concept of the *kingdom of God*. To preach the kingdom, as did Jesus during his personal ministry, is to preach the "rule" of God within human hearts. The things of the Spirit do not pertain to what is material and earthly, but to what is internal. They pertain to attitude and mind-set, to the intellectual decisions and emotional experiences of the inner man.

Whereas we often emphasize the church — the external, visible body of Christian people with it rules and rituals, Jesus' emphasis was on the *kingdom,* or "God's rule within the heart" of the individual. He recognized the place of the church, in fact, it is his creation and is the body of his people. The kingdom also is comprised of his followers, so it equates with the church in that respect, but it emphasizes the inwardness, the real faith and allegiance of the person's heart rather than the visible externals.

The fact of God's actually ruling in the human heart is not concerned with time or place or matter. It involves whether the person is surrendered, in submission and completely committed to Christ's will, so that his self-rule has been broken. The acceptance of God's rule means that it is to dominate in all our thinking and choices — social, intellectual, and spiritual.

The prayer, "Thy kingdom come" means the same thing as "Thy will be done." The kingdom is thought of here, then, as not the body of people, or a "territory" over which Christ rules, but as his dominion and lordship within each individual person. It is not "food and drink" but "righteousness and peace and joy in the Holy Spirit" (Rom. 14:17). We learn from 1 Corinthians 4:20 that the "kingdom of God does not consist in talk but in power." With the spiritual battle that we fight against Satan we need help, power of a spiritual nature from outside ourselves.

We need power to rescue us from the sin that we have become enmeshed in. We need power to help us overcome our everyday sins as pride, jealousy, and selfishness. We need power to help us positively — for forgiving, loving and helping our fellow man. When Christ's rule is operating in our hearts we can say no to Satan. We have needed strength because we no longer live unto ourselves, but unto God. We open ourselves to his help that comes through his teachings from his word, from his providential assistance and from his Spirit that indwells us.

When the kingdom or rule of God begins we have rejected self-rule, our hearts have been crushed, and we are in position for him to remold us as new creatures after his will. It is impossible for God's spiritual power to function in our lives if we have not yielded up ourselves and humbly submitted ourselves. As long as we want to "boss" our own lives and be our own masters we cannot be open to receive his power.

It costs to be a Christian. It costs all that we have. God's grace is expensive. We cannot be his and retain anything for ourselves. We cannot become a Christian with reservations.

Perhaps there are people who have "joined a church," thinking that they have gone all the way with Jesus, when in fact, they have never accepted his rule in their hearts, and so they are still wanting to serve two masters. They are still proud and ambitious in the wrong way, and were never really "converted." They do not realize what is wrong.

Such people need the preaching of God's rule (reign). It goes deeper than the outward and aims at the desires, the thoughts, and would change "the mind of the flesh" to "the mind of the Spirit." This would enable us to quit concentrating on a number of separate sins that we feel we must overcome ourselves one by one, and brings us to a "self-crucifixion" where we completely die to self and are raised to be one with Christ (see Rom. 6:4-9). God can take over when we make a complete surrender, and only then can we find true joy and peace.

Baptism is into God's rule or reign. All authority has been given to Jesus and when we are scripturally baptized into Christ (Gal. 3:27), we come under his controlling power. God adds such people to the church (Acts 2:47), but baptism is more than just for "church membership." It brings us under Christ's lordship and his authority. We are then under a new spiritual government, a new kingship, a new reign. We are his!

The Holy Spirit which indwells the Christian (Rom. 8:9) aids him in overcoming the "deeds of the body" (Rom. 8:13); he "leads" the Christian (v. 14); and he helps the Christian in his weaknesses (v. 26). We do not know how the Spirit functions in doing these things, but the fact that they are promised shows that a power for Christian living is available to God's persons. This, of course, is not "miraculous," as were the miracles and charismatic gifts of the first century, but it is *providential*, in that it is all done "behind the scenes." There are no "visible" or empirical supernatural demonstrations.

But the fact that *there is a power of God* in which the Christian's faith can be based, and that spiritual power is available for assisting us and bringing us blessings in the Christian life, should cause us to realize that *God has* meaningful *plans for us*. We are important to him. He loves us!

CHAPTER 32

THE CHRISTIAN'S SELF-ESTEEM

How valuable is the Christian person? In God's sight? In the sight of others? In one's own sight?

These are especially important questions for the adolescent as he (she) begins to bloom out into young manhood or young womanhood. He will be troubled until he "finds" himself — decides who he is and how important he is in the total picture of life. The day when any person learns "who he really is" and is willing to accept himself as he really is, is one of the great milestones of life. Obviously not everyone will be president of the United States (glory, honor, etc.), and of course not everyone will be a doormat for others to wipe their feet on. Therefore it behooves each of us to find our niche and accept it as adequate and important in God's scheme of things. To be sure there are one-talent people, two-talent people, and some five-talent people. If God has given us only one or two talents and we have learned this and are willing to accept it, knowing that we may however be "more victorious" in life than some of the five-talent people, we can be entirely happy with our lot. No one can be happy or content if he has an inferiority complex. Blessed is he who has found himself!

People who have found themselves and accept themselves as they really are make better husbands and wives. They can do better academically, and in coming to grips with the issues of life, because they are relaxed and are not constantly at odds with false concerns and fears. Young persons who "have their feet on the ground" and have already come to accept themselves at face value can also resist negative peer-influences better than others.

One major factor in being able to accept one's self is that of love. Man, as a person, has the capacity for and the need for love. Personalities become distorted if one does not feel loved. This is true of infants, of the aged, and every body in between! People cannot have a wholesome self-respect if they do not feel loved. But a sequel to that is that they also must love others. Love needs to flow both ways, else it cannot be maintained. The unloved person will in time lose his own self-respect, and may even become mentally sick. The normal life for God's person, especially for Christians who have been drawn into an awareness of God's love, is to be a person who expresses love for others freely, while at the same time realizing that he himself is freely loved, both by God and man.

God loves all mankind, so much so that he sent Jesus to die for us while we were yet sinners. He loves Christians especially, because they have responded to his "first-love" and have been born-again into his spiritual family. They are his children, in a beautiful relationship unknown to those who have rejected his "first-love."

Some indications from scripture that God loves us and counts each of us as very valuable among his creatures are:

Genesis 1:26, 27 - We were created to bear his image (Greek, *charakter*).

2 Peter 1:4 says that we can "become partakers of the divine nature." We are special creatures — the highest of all.

Genesis 1:26-28 - Man was given dominion over all other creatures and over all the earth. Man is important in God's sight.

Psalm 8:5, 6 - Man was made "a little less than God" himself. He was given glory and honor, and dominion.

Romans 5:9, 10 (also Rom. 3:24) - We were "bought back" (redeemed, reconciled) at great cost — by the shed blood of Christ himself. Surely God counted us important and worth saving by his willingness to permit Christ to die for us — this being the only hope at all for us, since there is no other effective atonement.

Psalm 91:11 (also Heb. 1:14) - God has directed angels to watch over us and guard us in our ways. Such indicates his feeling and concern for us.

John 14:1-3 - God has prepared mansions — proper dwelling places — for us in heaven. What other earthly creature does God make such provisions for?

From the above indications and any number of others that could be marshalled there can be no doubt that all human beings are important in God's sight. But this is even more true for his spiritual children, who recognize his existence and who revere his holy name. He is indeed their Father and Protector, and has promised that they shall inherit a glorious estate with him. He "works all things together" for them in a providential way in this life (Rom. 8:28), and has promised to "give us all things" needed for our spiritual good (Rom. 8:32). Indeed, God's children become "more than conquerors," with Christ's help, in the battles of life (Rom. 8:37). We are in fact "guaranteed" that this life will be a victory, if we maintain our faith.

No human being is unimportant. Even though there are some of us who have only one talent, we are just as important to God as the next person. Any one soul is more valuable than all the goods of this world.

It behooves each of us in the light of all this to yield ourselves to the Lord in faith and complete trust. We should love God, love our fellowman, and learn to love ourselves with a positive sense of self-importance. We *are* valuable! Then we should follow this new decision with some practical steps that will serve to keep us happy in God's grace.

1. Think positively, about ourselves and our potential.
2. Minimize all criticisms that come to us. There will be some, but it is a sign of maturity to take criticisms in stride, and change ourselves where we need to.
3. Believe that we can change for the better and can make a continuing growth.
4. Become involved in helping others. There are always people in worse condition than we are, and we will grow spiritually if we will lose ourselves in helping them.
5. Consciously keep ourselves yielded to God and to his providential ministrations. He is the potter, we are the clay.
6. Worship with God's other people regularly. Receive blessings from them and be a blessing to them, with the hope and the inspiration that we can furnish.
7. Forget all sense of competition with others. Be ourselves only. Do that well and God will make us succeed in all the right ways.

"For God so loved the world that he gave his only begotten Son, that whosoever believeth on him should not perish, but have everlasting life" (John 3:16).

GLOSSARY

ANTHROPOLOGY - A study of man

APOCRYPHA - The seven books included in the Catholic Old Testament but not in the Jewish or Protestant Old Testament

ARCHAEOLOGY - A scientific study of ancient things, especially as they pertain to the Bible (in our context)

AUTHORITY - One who has had empirical experience of something and thus a qualified to testify about it

CALVINISM - The Protestant faith promulgated by John Calvin which accents the Holy Spirit's actions, in election and guidance of the Christian

CANON - The list of books that make up the two Testaments

CONSERVATIVE - Theological stance that counts the Bible as God's authoritative word. Accepts the supernatural

COSMOLOGY - World view or total outlook upon the universe and its makeup

DETERMINISM - View that holds that man does not have free will. His actions are predetermined by physical causes

DISCREPANCIES - Mistakes or errors in the Bible. Accepted by Liberals but rejected by conservatives as existing in any problematic way

EMPIRICISM - Way of knowing through one or more of man's five senses

EVANGELICALS - Present-day conservatives in theology who also accept Calvinism (for the most part)

EXISTENTIALISM - Philosophical and theological stance which holds for subjectivity and denies reason as a valid way of arriving at religious knowledge

EXPERIENCE - Substitute term for Empiricism

FORM CRITICISM - A scientific study of "forms" or smaller units of biblical materials

FREE WILL - View that man has free moral choice, and responsibility

HIGHER CRITICISM - Scientific study of major areas of biblical concern, as authorship, dates, purposes, etc. Often done from the presupposition of philosophic naturalism

INERRANCY - Doctrine that the scriptures are without error (in the original manuscripts) in any significant way

INTUITION - Unmediated "way of knowing" theory held by some

LIBERAL, LIBERALISM - Theology with scientific approach and based on naturalistic presuppositions

LITERARY CRITICISM - A critical or scientific study of the biblical books as complete documents (as vs. "forms")

NATURALISM - Basic philosophical stance that denies supernatural activity as miracles, inspiration, etc., and holds for the laws of nature as being the ultimate

NEO-ORTHODOXY - A basically Existentialist theology

OBJECTIVITY - View which holds to realistic, public, objective facts that should form the basis of one's outlook

PHENOMENOLOGY - Philosophy that hopes to work out an objective study of values, or a "science of consciousness"

PHILOSOPHY - One's world view, total outlook or comprehensive view of the universe

PLENARY INSPIRATION - Theory that accepts the fact of supernatural production of the scriptures by the Holy Spirit without feeling obligated to choose how it may have been accomplished

REASON - Man's normal faculty of logic used (in our context) to evaluate facts and evidence and arrive at a truth conclusion

SCIENTIFIC METHOD - A precise program of reasoning upon

a problem by using the inductive method of reasoning, higher mathematics, precise measurements and careful thoroughness

SUBJECTIVITY - Private knowledge, known "internally" and non-communicable, such as: Values - good, beauty, love and similar metaphysical realities

TEXTUAL CRITICISM - Study of variants and ultimately to arrive at the original

TEXTUAL VARIANTS - Differences between two manuscripts of the same text

WORLD VIEW - Same as "Cosmology." Total outlook on the universe

SUBJECT INDEX